T0279903

PRAISE FOR

PRAISE FOR
Insubordinate

"I am so glad Jocelyn Davis has finally written the book on female leadership archetypes. There has been far too little conversation on the ways women lead, even when they do not have formal power. Davis dives deep into her repertoire of real, fictional, and mythological women to help us understand the many different styles that have matched different situations in time. You will recognize yourself here; I, for one, found myself in the water-earth quadrant. To recognize yourself is to own your strengths and ultimately to have the freedom to move beyond them."

Dr. Shalini Lal, Founder and CEO, Unqbe; coauthor of *The Secret Life of Organizations*

"In her exciting new book filled with stories classic and contemporary, Jocelyn Davis offers women a way to think expansively about ourselves: our personalities, talents, and opportunities. 'Lean in' becomes leaning into our strengths and appreciating others' strengths. 'Move up' becomes moving freely and deciding where we want to go. Too often, we women feel we need to meet expectations and say yes to everything, but the truth is, we can say no and follow our joy. *Insubordinate* empowers us to do just that."

Dr. Beverly Kaye, coauthor of *Wall Street Journal* bestsellers *Love 'em or Lose 'em* and *Up Is Not the Only Way*

"Joseph Campbell started a conversation for all of us about how we encounter the heroic journey of personal transformation. Now, Jocelyn Davis expands the conversation with thoughtful theory, engaging stories, and practical how-tos that are particularly relevant for today's women. Davis inspires us to be our best and bravest self and to give full expression to the female hero in each us."

Susan Chamberlin, Director, Joseph Campbell Foundation

"*Insubordinate* is a book I wish I'd had access to when I was coming of age and one that I am thrilled women of all ages will have access to now. Jocelyn Davis turns her razor wit and keen eye to women, women's work, and women's stories and in so doing reveals twelve archetypes that point to powerful leadership qualities found in unexpected places. What does the Snow Queen have to show us about what it takes to lead? How does the Witch take initiative? These are just some of the tantalizing questions Davis answers in a book that centers women and what we have been doing forever: leading, each in our own unique way. Highly recommended!"

Briana Saussy, author of *Making Magic* and *Star Child: Joyful Parenting Through Astrology*

"I keep coming back to Davis's books because she finds a way to write in a historically fascinating way while unearthing self-insights that other business writers don't. This latest offering will start you reading to find out which archetype you are, but it will keep you reading to learn how your place intersects with that of other women, as well as men; how deep the cultural rules go, and why you have adapted the way you have; and most important, how you can become a more well-rounded, richer person on this planet. Enjoy the emotional and illustrative journey."

Dr. Kelly Kinnebrew, organizational psychologist; Founder, MinervaCoach

"Intriguing! I love the stories, which made me reflect on my own experience. Besides being a very good read, *Insubordinate* is a practical self-development guidebook for women at different points in their careers. I will recommend it to my network and our students."

Carol Zheng, Regional Director, Executive Education Business and Partnership Development, Ivey Business School Asia

"A fascinating look into the multiple roles that women play and the facets that make them who they are. Drawing on the premise that a woman's greatest strength is her range, Davis weaves together stories from mythology, literature, and real life to explore the archetypes that influence the complex, shape-shifting, and multitasking lives of women. *Insubordinate* is a treasure map for men to understand, respect, and appreciate the women in their lives and a field guide for women to lead effectively by expanding their repertoire and breaking free. A captivating, articulate, and elegant masterclass in constructive insubordination!"

Sumeet Shetty, President, Literati: India's largest corporate book club

"*Insubordinate* pulls back the tent flap on the elemental qualities of a woman's way of leading. Davis brings an anthropological lens to female leadership through archetypes and their alignments with the qualities of fire, water, earth, and air, pointing us to strengths unique to women leaders: range, mutability, and versatility. She redraws the definition of leadership to highlight the feminine capacity for context awareness, leading in 3-D, and fluid expansion of repertoire rather than linear march to the goal."

Dr. Molly McGinn, anthropologist; Founder and Managing Partner, TreeHouse Learning Community

"Understanding oneself is fundamental to leadership. This clever book takes readers on a journey of self-discovery, enlightening us with fanciful characters and stories that magically help us realize our own leadership capacities and gifts."

Janine Mason, Founder, Fieldstone Leadership Network San Diego

"I loved the point that women are shape-shifters. Instead of seeing ourselves as just one archetype, our true strength and influence comes when we realize we have access to all the archetypes and apply them accordingly."

Carmelita Lubos, Chief People Officer, HealthHero

"There are many ways for the feminine to express power and presence. When we turn toward archetype, we connect with a power that is both within us and larger than us. Davis has codified a wheel of feminine archetypes of leadership to guide us in accessing this power. She takes us into the realm of myth (where all archetypes come from) and brings us back down to earth with real stories of leadership. Under her guidance, we are liberated from the prejudice of female stereotypes and empowered to find and claim our expression of feminine leadership. A natural storyteller, Davis takes the tone of a close girlfriend letting you in on some juicy gossip—that has a deeper purpose."

Daven Lee, Founder, The Yin Center

"Do you ever feel stuck in a certain pattern of behavior or way of being in the world? Well, who doesn't? *Insubordinate* will help you get unstuck. Davis makes a powerful argument: 'Women's greatest strength is our range.' Pack this book in your knapsack and let it guide you on the lifelong path to realize the many dimensions of your potential."

Paul Hellman, author of *You've Got 8 Seconds: Communication Secrets for a Distracted World*; Founder, Express Potential®

"With over three decades in corporate America, I have encountered every one of these twelve archetypes. It's refreshing to see a feminine-focused framework for leadership, and I recommend this book for anyone who would like insight into how women can overcome stereotypes, build on their strengths, and expand their influence. A fun and informative read."

Rosie Mucklo, Head of Underwriting University, Zurich North America

"Davis's latest book is a captivating, mind-expanding read that provides insight, inspiration, and life examples to transform how you lead and how you think about women in leadership."

Cynthia Stuckey, SVP Growth, LHH/Ezra

"For too long I have struggled as a woman in business and life because I've tried to obey and comply. I've made who I am subordinate to the path I was trying to forge; I've discarded the parts of me that I thought weren't important. Finally I figured out I was failing because there was 'too much left behind of the rest of me.' I had discounted and discarded my gifts. If I'd had this framework of women's archetypes then, I'd have found a way ahead far faster and with less suffering for all concerned. *Insubordinate* held me in thrall from the quiz on the first page to the do's and don'ts on the last page, helping me to figure out who I am, understand and value each facet, and delight in the congruence and wholeness I feel when I pull the pieces together. Here is the call to action for any and every woman to embrace and use her gifts even if they aren't in line with the current regime. If you want to know what it feels like to be free of the self-limiting beliefs that hold you back, this is the book for you."

Vivien Price, Solution Architect, FranklinCovey

"Jocelyn Davis brings a fresh perspective to women at work (and women in general) by suggesting that instead of adopting the cookie-cutter persona of the 'woman of the moment,' we engage our unique traits to achieve success. Davis does what she does best: skillfully weaves ancient tales with modern-day situations to demonstrate that the stories she shares are as alive and relevant today as they were at their inception. She contends that although we may have natural tendencies, they do not define us; the beauty of women is in how they choose to be. She presents each archetype not as a life sentence but as a springboard allowing women the freedom to choose from a range of gifts, thereby gaining strength beyond our comprehension. But we must learn to use these gifts appropriately, and Davis shows us how. *Insubordinate* is for any woman who wants to succeed because of who she is, not despite it."

Sabina Sulat, author of *Agile Unemployment*

ALSO BY JOCELYN DAVIS

Strategic Speed

The Greats on Leadership

The Art of Quiet Influence

The Age of Kali: A Novel

Insubordinate

12 New Archetypes
for Women Who Lead

JOCELYN DAVIS

ILLUSTRATIONS BY INBAR FRIED

amplify
an imprint of Amplify Publishing Group

www.amplifypublishing.com

Insubordinate: 12 New Archetypes for Women Who Lead

Author's Note: I have changed all personal names and some company details in order to protect anonymity. The real-life stories are as I remember them or as they were told to me; others will no doubt remember them differently.

The views and opinions expressed in this book are solely those of the author. These views and opinions do not necessarily represent those of the publisher or staff.

Illustrations by Inbar Fried
Design by Caitlin Smith

For more information, please contact:

Amplify Publishing, an imprint of Amplify Publishing Group
620 Herndon Parkway, Suite 320
Herndon, VA 20170
info@amplifypublishing.com

Library of Congress Control Number: 2022907679

CPSIA Code: PRV0922A

ISBN-13: 978-1-63755-387-9

Printed in the United States

For Maggie, Beth, and Kate,
my insubordinate inspirations

CONTENTS

You find yourself in a messy conflict with a couple of coworkers. You:

- **A.** Confront them head-on
- **B.** Try to get them on your side
- **C.** Avoid them as much as possible
- **D.** Find ways to outshine them

Your best traits are your:

- **A.** Boldness and enthusiasm
- **B.** Quiet ability to get along with anyone
- **C.** Cool head and steady approach
- **D.** Sense of command and creativity

In meetings, you tend to:

- **A.** Advocate for swift action; why sit around talking?
- **B.** Support and amplify others' ideas
- **C.** Listen, reflect, and take notes
- **D.** Play devil's advocate and/or make people laugh

Sometimes you can be too:

- **A.** Outspoken
- **B.** Compromising
- **C.** Perfectionistic
- **D.** Bossy

Your sense of humor is:

- **A.** Boisterous
- **B.** Gentle
- **C.** Wry
- **D.** Sharp

Your idea of a fun evening is:

- **A.** A hot date at a dive bar
- **B.** A great play or concert
- **C.** Home alone with a book
- **D.** Something unique, arranged by you

QUIZ: WHAT'S YOUR ARCHETYPE?

You're a good friend because you are:
- **A.** Forthright and fun
- **B.** Warm and congenial
- **C.** Calm and understanding
- **D.** Smart and offbeat

Your favorite films tend to be:
- **A.** Action-adventure movies
- **B.** Romantic comedies
- **C.** Thoughtful dramas
- **D.** Sci-fi or horror flicks

You've been assigned to lead an important project. Your first concern is to:
- **A.** Build enthusiasm and commitment to the mission
- **B.** Help the team set ground rules to ensure smooth collaboration
- **C.** Step back, assess the situation, and make a plan
- **D.** Establish your authority and lay out a clear vision of success

Of these Disney characters, you identify most with:
- **A.** Mulan (*Mulan*)
- **B.** Ariel (*The Little Mermaid*)
- **C.** Elsa (*Frozen*)
- **D.** All the "wicked queens"

Your career goals are mostly about:
- **A.** Being a fighter for...
- **B.** Being of service to...
- **C.** Being independent from...
- **D.** Being in charge of...

Which one of these color combinations is most you?
- **A.** Fire red and earth brown
- **B.** Earth brown and water green
- **C.** Water green and sky blue
- **D.** Sky blue and fire red

Note the number of As, Bs, Cs, and Ds in your answers:

A _____   B _____

C _____   D _____

Interpretation

Use the Archetypes Wheel to interpret your results:

- **Mostly As:** Fire-earth quadrant (southeast)

- **Mostly Bs:** Earth-water quadrant (southwest)

- **Mostly Cs:** Water-air quadrant (northwest)

- **Mostly Ds:** Air-fire quadrant (northeast)

- **Mostly As and Bs:** The earth types (south)

- **Mostly Bs and Cs:** The water types (west)

- **Mostly Cs and Ds:** The air types (north)

- **Mostly Ds and As:** The fire types (east)

- **Any other combination:** Read on to learn more about the archetypes and decide which ones are most truly you.

Archetypes Wheel

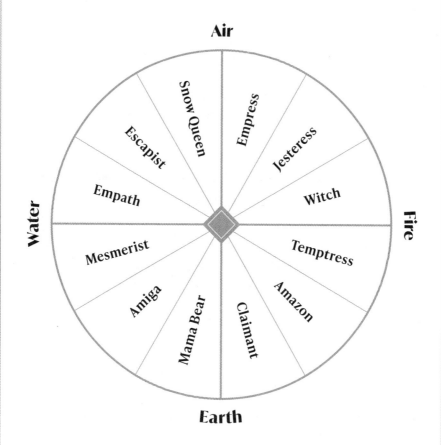

We teach girls to shrink themselves, to make themselves smaller.
Chimamanda Ngozi Adichie

We must smuggle back to other women our plundered treasures.
Mary Daly

There is, after all, much to be said for leaning out.
Rosa Brooks

THE HEROINE'S JOURNEY

WOMAN IS BORN FREE, yet everywhere she is in chains.

That's the first line of *The Social Contract* by French philosopher Jean-Jacques Rousseau—except he wrote, "*Man* is born free, yet everywhere *he* is in chains." Rousseau pictures primitive men living in a state of delightful ease: lounging under trees, picking fruit to satisfy their hunger, having sex, singing songs, and generally enjoying themselves without need for kings or laws, jobs or money, governments or wars. What requires explaining, Rousseau says, is the state we find ourselves in today: encumbered not only by laws, money, and wars, but also by endless, grueling competition for status and resources. How did we go from that early Eden to today's rat race? he wonders. *The Social Contract* is his attempt to reconstruct the journey in order to discover a way of shaking our bonds, or at least learning to live with them.

I've stolen and changed Rousseau's opening line because this book is also about freedom—but not for men. This book is about freedom for women, who both want it more than men and have a harder time getting it. Men, I maintain, were never the idle, noncompetitive creatures of Rousseau's imagination, nor were they the savage brutes some others envision; men have always been natural hierarchs and conformists, wearing society's chains with the pride of a knight for his armor or a soldier for his medals. Men are at home in pyramids. Women, in contrast, resist man-made power structures: sure, we'll bend the knee because it's necessary for survival, but we never bow as readily as the guys do. Whenever you see a group of men lined up to salute a flag or captain, there's sure to be a group of women somewhere off to the side, grinding corn for the day's bread as they talk, laugh, and plot rebellions. For us women, the shackles of the system are a nuisance at best, a torture at worst. We are, by nature and necessity, insubordinate.

Too often, however, we waste our insubordinate strength. Underestimating our potential for leadership, we keep our ambitions contained, our attempts to throw off the chains tentative. To break those chains, we cannot stay small. We must become big—by which I don't mean loud and aggressive (though sometimes that might be required) or possessed of a fancy title or high position. By *big*, I mean "able to embrace the full scope of women's ways of leading."

Women's greatest strength vis-à-vis men is our *range*. We are shapeshifters, multitaskers, jacks (or Jacquelines) of all trades who across times and cultures have been pleased to say, in the words of the Peggy Lee song turned ad jingle, "I can bring home the bacon, fry it up in a pan, and nevernever-never let you forget you're a man." Sexist claptrap? Maybe, but it points to a profound truth: women contain multitudes. While men lead by setting their sights on a goal and marching straight for it (a hero's journey, if you will), we women lead by expanding our repertoire: by becoming the opera diva equally brilliant in the role of gentle Madama Butterfly, warlike Brünnhilde, proud Isolde, or vivacious Carmen. In Shakespeare's *Antony and Cleopatra*, a soldier says of the famous Egyptian queen, "Age cannot wither her, nor custom stale her infinite variety." It's a tribute that may apply to any of us.*

---

* Some feminist thinkers believe men would be better off if they, too, cultivated a wider range. I agree that many men would benefit from greater fluidity in behavior and presentation (and I hope my male readers pick up some tips), but I see no need for men to abandon their linear focus, which humanity needs, too. Think of

The following pages contain stories of twelve insubordinate women who fought, cajoled, commanded, schemed, or blasted their way free of the chains that bound them. Each of the twelve represents a different approach to work and life; each taken alone is incomplete, but taken together, they show us woman's complete repertoire—our "infinite variety"—providing a guide and inspiration for our heroine's journey. The stories are old; some, thousands of years old. I believe that classic myths and legends are where we find the best models for becoming more than we are. Of course there are plenty of inspiring women in the real world today, and I'll be telling some of their stories, too. Unfortunately, what the real world mostly offers are examples of women being less than they can be.

This is not our fault. "We teach girls to shrink themselves, to make themselves smaller," says activist Chimamanda Ngozi Adichie in her TED talk; moreover, women as a class face heavy burdens—unequal pay, unequal education, domestic violence, and rape as a tool of war, to name just a few—which can crush us down no matter how big we manage to make ourselves (and which are even heavier for women of color, gender nonconforming women, and lower-income women). This book, however, will not be a treatise on systemic misogyny, for plenty of others have written on that topic. I take systemic misogyny, like systemic racism, as a given: everywhere, women are in chains. My question is: What are we going to do about it?

Let's begin by considering the insubordinate woman's number-one pitfall, which I call the Medusa Trap. Here's a true story that illustrates it.

Five Medusas by the Pool

April 2011. At lunch break, we five executives—all female, all friends—navigated the buffet line then carried our plates outside to a glass-topped table on the far side of the hotel pool. With sunglasses perched on our noses,

---

the words of Todd Beamer on 9/11 as he prepared to charge up the aisle of United Airlines Flight 93: "Let's roll."

pashminas draped on the arms of our chairs, we sat and ate and complained about our new boss, who had called the management meeting currently underway. The Florida air was hot and humid. The light breeze over the water was refreshing.

"*What* was up with that thing he drew on the flipchart this morning?" said Liz, a regional vice president. "That weird picture of the guy with the big ears and tiny mouth."

Margaret, the in-house counsel, dabbed her mouth with a paper napkin and said in a voice dripping sarcasm: "He's listening more than he talks, see. It's a metaphor."

"Wow. Creative," said Liz. Margaret chuckled.

"But seriously," I said, stabbing a bit of penne, "this meeting is ridiculous. He says he wants ideas for the reorg, but we know the decisions have already been made."

Amanda, head of Global Sales, pushed a long blonde lock behind her ear and frowned. Normally she was circumspect, but now she wasn't bothering to hide her anger: "Exactly. I mean he can make those decisions, he's the boss, but why is he pretending to involve us when it's already a done deal? That's what gets me."

Laurie, another regional VP, was blunt as usual: "It's completely unethical. You realize he's already decided who's getting laid off. Not to mention the money we're wasting on this meeting. Flying us all down here. There goes everyone's bonus, quite frankly."

There was a pause as we sipped from our water bottles.

"Oh, hey," I said, "you guys never told us about what happened last Friday. The team dinner. C'mon, let's hear it."

Amanda and Margaret looked at each other and rolled their eyes. There ensued a story told by Amanda, with many interjections from Margaret, about how our new president had tromped through the New York office late Friday afternoon, ignoring people's protests as he interrupted their client calls, and dragged everyone off to his favorite restaurant where he proceeded to order an array of meat dishes then chide the vegetarians when they declined to eat. As the two raconteurs acted out the gaffes, mimicking people's facial expressions, we could hardly contain ourselves. For the next five minutes we had good laughs at our boss's expense.

Then the boss appeared.

I saw him emerge from the hotel side door: lunch plate in hand, an affable smile on his face, he strode toward us around the edge of the pool. I elbowed Amanda; she and I began to make those throaty hums universally recognized as danger signals. We all stopped talking.

"May I join you?" He pulled up a chair.

"Sure."

"Please."

"Of course."

The scene that followed was cringeworthy. Victor (as I'll call him) was trying to be pleasant, but his attempts fell flat. Whether it was because of his different cultural background or simply his personality, he had since his start date seemed uncomfortable with our very American, very feminine norms of relaxed collegiality. Our organization—indeed, our entire industry—was predominantly women, which meant power displays didn't go down well; male new-hires learned quickly to drop the bluster and make nice with the ladies. Victor grasped the concept and tried to fit in, but playing the jovial equal didn't come naturally to him.

Now, as he peppered us with questions about how we thought the meeting was going and whether we had any input for him, our hostility was palpable. We knew he had already made all the decisions the meeting was supposed to address—or rather, had had those decisions dictated to him by *his* manager, the Big Boss—and that the whole thing was therefore a sham. His pretense at openness only made us angrier.

"What did you think of the team report-outs?" he asked, munching his tuna sandwich.

A long pause.

"I thought there were some good ideas," I said.

"What did you like, especially?"

Another long pause.

"Everyone seems very engaged," said Liz, toying with her bracelet.

"Any feedback for me?"

Bland smiles. Bland shrugs.

After several more minutes of this, Victor gave up and launched into a monologue. He expounded on the company strategy, the need for innovation, the challenges we faced, and the heroic things he'd done to drive growth at his previous organization. He made no mention of the upcoming layoffs. As he spoke on, we regarded him blank-faced: the disks of our sunglasses flat, dark, implacable. The strands of our hair waved in the breeze.

You've heard the myth of Medusa, the snake-haired monster whose gaze turned men to stone. That day we were five Medusas, eyeing with monstrous disdain the man who had come unbidden to our island. Under our Gorgon gaze, Victor's manner grew more awkward, his speech more halting, until finally he fell silent and applied himself again to his sandwich; whereupon Amanda, gathering her purse and pashmina, said, "Sorry, I have to get an email off to a client." There was a general murmur about urgent tasks we, too, had only just remembered we needed to complete, and with apologies we rose and departed, leaving Victor to finish his lunch alone.

Perhaps you feel sorry for him; after all, the business decisions had been imposed on him from above. And at least he was courteous. Overall, though, Victor wasn't much of a leader—really just a pile of ego—so I can't blame us for rejecting his overtures and, six months later, driving him out.

Oh yes; we drove him out. Toward the end of the year, with the numbers not looking good, several of us on the leadership team complained about Victor to the Big Boss, who, taking a step perhaps already contemplated, gave him the boot. Our male peers at senior levels gave their opinions when asked, but they were not the instigators; they had been toeing the line and only now joined in, gingerly, with the female rebellion. On the day Victor's departure was announced, with the mood throughout the company celebratory, my colleagues and I went out and raised a glass to freedom. I in particular was eager to take credit for dispatching the tyrant.

And things were good for a while. But before long there arrived another boss who was worse than Victor in every way, and there began a downward slide, which accelerated through multiple layoffs and firings, multiple CEOs, and multiple attempts to reverse the decline, ending a decade later with the once-proud company, now a sliver of its former self, merging without a ripple into a vast corporate sea. We five Medusas had scattered long ago, paddling our lifeboats away to other islands.

Breaking Free: The Advice Women Get

The Medusa Trap is women's tendency to squander our natural insubordination on petty displays of spite directed at our enemies, real or perceived; some call it "toxic femininity." While it can feel good to see a blowhard frozen by our disdain, and while we might imagine it makes us powerful, the Gorgon's gaze is really just a female version of the chest-thumping we find so pathetic in men: just a mean girl's way to puff herself up, creating an illusion of power. And like chest-thumping, it's effective only in minor, temporary ways. My friends and I achieved nothing valuable or lasting with our poolside snark or our management coup.

The original Medusa was decapitated by Perseus, who avoided her deadly gaze by looking at her reflection in his magic shield. Feminist scholars note that Medusa got a raw deal: the goddess Athena turned her into a Gorgon as punishment for being raped in Athena's own temple, then banished her to an island where she was pursued by trophy hunters and eventually killed. It's a sad and uninspiring story, for a Gorgon lady has but one act in her repertoire: the withering, shriveling stare. When we emulate her, we only make ourselves smaller.*

So what are the better models?

There's no shortage of advice out there: professional, personal, and spiritual. Much of it is useful, but none of it is fully satisfying. Let's take a quick look at the four main types of advice served up by the modern-day gurus of

---

* There are other ways to interpret the myth of Medusa; for example, it could be seen as a tale of one woman (Athena) helping another (Medusa) to escape her abuser. Medusa's head ends up on Athena's war shield, the famous Aegis that protects the city of Athens. Looked at thus, she is a symbol of female power and solidarity.

female empowerment: (1) lean in, (2) aim to please, (3) walk the tightrope, and (4) work together for change.

1. Lean in. Sheryl Sandberg's book of this name is the best-known in a large collection of similar guides that urge women to be more assured and direct—to "sit at the table," as Sandberg puts it, rather than in a side chair. Some of these advisers take a kindly big-sister tone: be confident, don't sell yourself short, I'm rooting for you. Others are more in the tough-love vein: it's a man's world and the men play hardball, so quitcher whining and learn to play hardball yourself. Some say this type of counsel is geared to rich women with household help and super-supportive husbands, a criticism that seems justified: if you're a single mom who has to pick up the kids at daycare then pull a second shift of dinner prep, homework, baths, bedtime, and a couple more hours of email, laundry, and worrying about the bills before finally getting to sleep after midnight, you're not going to have much energy left for rocking the morning meeting.

But the larger problem with this category of advice isn't the elitist myopia; it's the assumption that climbing a corporate ladder is the only game in town *and* that the rules of that game must always be followed. Of course the lean-in proponents will counter that if climbing a corporate ladder isn't your thing, their book isn't for you. By anchoring their advice in corporate structures, however, they overlook the many paths for women that involve dodging or subverting those structures even while operating within or alongside them. As you'll see, many of my real-world examples of female archetypes engaged in just that sort of subversion: they played a man's game, not by his rules. Or they stepped out of the game altogether. Leaning in is fine, but (to quote Georgetown law professor Rosa Brooks) there is much to be said for leaning out.[1]

2. Aim to please. These advisers would have us drop all attempts at hardball and instead work to become, in the words of Marabel Morgan's bestselling book of 1973, a "total woman." The original total woman was a homemaker who'd go to any lengths to please her husband, whether by flattering him, cooking his favorite meals, or (as the author famously suggested) greeting him at the door in the evening wearing nothing but three Dixie Cups. *The Total Woman* lifted to prominence an entire self-help genre focused on techniques for finding, catching, and keeping a successful male partner. Dating and marriage are the main topics, but there's also a subgenre that counsels women in the workplace to soften their approach and polish their appearance in order to form alliances with men who'll look out for them professionally. I remember reading about one women's workshop—I don't recall the sponsor—at which attendees were instructed to wear "the three Ps: pink, pumps, and pearls" in order to assure their advancement at the office. (Again we see the bias toward women who can afford pearls.)

Morgan and her ilk are easy to mock, but their advice isn't crazy. They believe in gender complementarity: that men and women have different natures entailing different strengths, and that we should play to those strengths. The concept of a "female brain," though questioned by most neuro-scientists, crops up often in the sort of book that may not tell women to wear the three Ps but does tell them to use their supposedly superior teamwork abilities, listening skills, or empathy in order to stand out from the men and get ahead. Again, not crazy. The drawback of this type of advice, though, is that "strong and complementary" can easily devolve into "weak and lesser." A badass woman *can* wear pink, pumps, and pearls, but at some point she's likely to find those heels slowing her down. (Not to mention the Dixie Cups.)

3. Walk the tightrope. The so-called tightrope dilemma is the need to walk the line between competence and likability. It's a balance easy for men to strike, hard for women. Research shows that a man perceived as competent tends also to be perceived as likable, while the more competent a woman seems the less likable she seems, and the more likable, the less competent.* A competent woman pursuing a higher position is especially apt to be disliked; once she achieves the higher position (if she achieves it) and starts actually doing the job, her competence and likability are easier

---

* For an overview of research on the tightrope dilemma, see *What Works for Women at Work,* by Joan C. Williams and Rachel Dempsey.

for people to reconcile. Gurus therefore suggest we walk the tightrope by, basically, disguising our ambition: smile a lot, act friendly, tout our team's accomplishments rather than our own, say "we" not "I," and never, ever let on that we aspire to the boss's job. In other words, go ahead and be competent—just don't act like we expect to be rewarded for it.

This genre of advice acknowledges the shortcomings of "lean in" and "aim to please" and tries to combine the two approaches into one, whereby we project a perfect balance of strength and warmth while cleverly hiding our will to power. It's a sophisticated take on what works for women; the problem is that balancing acts are exhausting. Who can walk a tightrope all day, every day? Thinking back on my own attempts to do it over a 25-year consulting career, I can see that although I often succeeded, it was only because I was lucky enough to work in a place unusually supportive of women. As I've mentioned, our company's senior staff was mostly female; moreover, the company founder (a man) had made it his explicit aim to create a woman-friendly culture. That culture lasted as long as a home-grown CEO was in charge, but when a new regime took over, I was shocked to see how quickly the tightrope got yanked out from under us women leaders, our balancing acts no longer effective or appreciated.

4. Work together for change. By now you might be getting irritated. "Why should women have to worry about any of this stuff?" you ask. "Why must we modify *our* behavior to accommodate the world's misogyny? Isn't all this advice—lean in, aim to please, walk the tightrope—just like telling women not to wear skimpy clothing so they don't get raped? How about instead of blaming the victims, we tell the rapists to stop raping?"

Many feminist thinkers argue the same. No amount of leaning in or wearing pink, they say, will accomplish the real goal, which is to shatter the patriarchal systems that oppress women, especially lower-income women and women of color. To do that, we need to organize. We need to work together to change regressive laws, get more women into positions of power, and provide them with access to the resources they need in order to rise out of poverty, control their bodies, get an education, and escape danger. Once that work is accomplished, these feminists go on to say, there will be no further need for tips on how to succeed at the office or how to avoid being raped. There will be a level playing field on which women will compete as equals. Women will be free, and women will thrive.

To that I say: Yes, by all means, let's work for structural change; several of the archetypes inspire just this sort of effort. Once again, though, this good advice is incomplete advice, for the advocates of structural change have nothing to say about what we're supposed to do while we're waiting for the great day of freedom and equality to arrive. "Go on working for change," they say. Fine, but that doesn't help me deal with my difficult boss *today*. It doesn't help me get a promotion so I can pay my bills *today*. It doesn't help me decide whether to leave my abusive partner *today*. It doesn't help me cope with my dysfunctional family or my toxic friend or my own destructive habits—*today*.

Every problem is immediate and personal to somebody. The tips we women share in order to help one another with our immediate, personal problems are, I believe, every bit as worthwhile as the marches and rallies, petitions and phone banks. When one of my first managers (a woman) told me to uncross my arms and smile so I'd come across friendlier, that wasn't oppressive nonsense; it was useful feedback. When I told my college-age daughter not to get blind drunk at parties lest she be sexually assaulted, that wasn't blaming the victim; it was sound counsel on how to enhance (note well, I do not say *assure*) her safety, counsel that was entirely compatible with my donations to RAINN and advocacy for tougher laws against human trafficking.

To repeat: Women's greatest strength in our ongoing struggle for freedom is our range. We can march for justice *and* sit at the table *and* walk a tight-rope—wearing pink, if necessary. If pink doesn't work, we can try blue, or chartreuse, or purple polka dots. Mutability is our magic. Divergence is our deal. Is it fair that we face so many barriers? Of course not. But even as we acknowledge the unfairness, we should never forget there is plenty we can do, individually and together, to leap, dodge, crawl under, smash, or otherwise defeat the barriers. Despite the many forces conspiring to keep us small, we can be big.

Twelve Archetypes for Women

Ancient sages believed that the world we experience can be reduced to a small set of irreducible elements. The Persian mystic Zoroaster proposed four: fire, water, earth, and air. The Greek philosopher Aristotle added a fifth: aether, or void. Other ancient cultures, including Babylonia, India, Tibet, and Japan, had similar lists; the Chinese included wood and metal in theirs. The Greeks saw the elements as material substances. The Hindus associated them with the five senses. And in China, they were and still are considered to be energies in cosmology, astrology, and the art of auspicious arrangement known as feng shui. Although Western science long ago replaced them with the elements of the periodic table, the four classical elements have continued to resonate in the art, literature, and spiritual practices of West and East. Here are some of their associations:

- **Fire:** hot, direct, attacking, bright, external, visible
- **Water:** cool, indirect, yielding, dark, internal, invisible
- **Earth:** down, heavy, steady, emotional, practical, flesh
- **Air:** up, light, mercurial, intellectual, abstract, mind

Fire and water are opposites, as are earth and air. When we array the four elements on a wheel, we get four quadrants: fire-earth, earth-water, water-air, and air-fire (see figure 1). Within each quadrant are three archetypes: twelve archetypes in all.* Let's briefly consider them.

Fire-earth: The lower right quadrant is home to passionate women who come on strong and don't back down; who, whether grappling with an adversary

---

* An archetype is a recurrent symbol, image, theme, or character that represents a universal aspect of human nature. Psychologist C. G. Jung proposed seven "feminine archetypes": Maiden, Mother, Huntress, Wise Woman (or Sage), Wild Woman (or Mystic), Queen, and Lover. I propose twelve, based on the four classical elements. Each of my twelve archetypes represents a woman's way of being—an option for women, if you will. They are based not in modern science, but rather in literature, folklore, art, spiritual traditions, and human experience.

or selling an idea, do it frontally, fiercely, with no time for picky analysis or girlish vagaries. The *Temptress* directs relationship energy toward men and women alike, captivating them with her spicy daredevilry. The *Amazon* is a confident, happy warrior, charging full force into hot conflicts. The *Claimant*, sure of her rights and rightness, plants her feet and declares, "Here I stand."

Earth-water: The lower left quadrant is the realm of the subtle, smiling woman, the woman who wields influence softly and darkly: giving way as necessary, casting a veil over her intentions, knowing that the greatest victory is that which requires no battle. The *Mama Bear* is an earth goddess whose power flows through her "children," be they of her family or her team. The *Amiga* is a mistress of alignment who can make an ally at the drop of a hat. The *Mesmerist* seduces with words and images, leaving her audience wanting more.

Figure 1: Archetypes Wheel

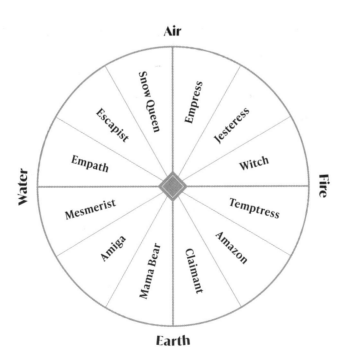

Water-air: The upper left quadrant is where we find the cool, crystalline dream girls: the ones who hold themselves aloof, who sail serenely through stormy seas, whose powers of evasion are surpassed only by their aura of calm. The *Empath*, as her name indicates, personifies empathy, mercy, and understanding, though she dispenses them dispassionately. The *Escapist*, opposite of the Amazon, is an artful dodger who keeps her head down when fights heat up. The *Snow Queen*, icy, strong, and proud, strives to rise above the mucky world.

Air-fire: At the upper right we have the dedicated achievers and brilliant talkers, the women who use their keen intellects and sharp tongues to outmaneuver adversaries, attract followers, and deconstruct barriers. The *Empress* is a commander, masculine in her ambition and drive; she takes charge to achieve her goals. The *Jesteress*, born under a merry star, uses rapier wit to deflect attacks and skewer pomposity. Finally, there's the *Witch*: most reviled of the twelve archetypes, she flouts convention and often pays a heavy price.

These archetypes are *timeless* in that they have been around for millennia, but *new* in that no one until now has identified them, arranged them thus, and showed how they can inspire women leaders. For a preview of how we'll explore them, see table 1: Contents Map.

Table 1: Contents Map

Archetype	Literary Example	Real-life Example	How to Emulate Her
1. Temptress	Carmen	Caroline, a marketing executive and CEO	Make people feel special Bring the fun Let them see you like them
2. Amazon	Lysistrata	Lacey, a small-company founder	Know what you want Find allies Be sure in your rightness Fight with good intent

Archetype	Literary Example	Real-life Example	How to Emulate Her
3. Claimant	Shakuntala	Shauna, a project manager turned salesperson	Strengthen your BATNA Play by the rules
4. Mama Bear	Rebekah	Renee, a regional executive	Identify with your team's success Treat them differently Take the blame
5. Amiga	Savitri	Sabrina, a graduate student and teaching assistant	See relationships in two dimensions (friend or foe, ally or adversary)
6. Mesmerist	Shahrazade	Cheryl, a salesperson	Persist . . . nicely Emphasize larger goals Give your audience space
7. Empath	Guanyin	Wendy, a nurse	Listen and confirm Err toward generosity Be an objective eye
8. Escapist	Penelope	Pam, a consultant	Disengage Learn to say "No" Embrace the gift of fear
9. Snow Queen	Isolde	Isabel, a college student, later a product designer	Expect commitment Focus on results Keep calm and carry on
10. Empress	Lady Macbeth	Amanda, a sales executive	Respect the hierarchy Speak with conviction Push for your purpose Lean in—literally
11. Jesteress	Sei Shonagon	Zara, a foreign-service wife and mother	Take fights lightly Say "Yes, and . . ." Be brief
12. Witch	Medea	Maddie, a writer and spiritualist	Be judiciously ruthless Heal the rifts

Some Hollywood Examples

One way to see the archetypes in action is to study Hollywood films with a strong female lead and a plotline that may be summarized as "starts one-dimensional, ends multidimensional"; I call it the heroine's journey. The popularity of such films is testament to the enduring power and appeal of this journey and the myths it draws on. Here are five examples.*

Legally Blonde: California good-time girl and marriage hopeful Elle Woods is a cute but insipid combination of blonde-bimbo Temptress and air-headed Amiga. When her boyfriend dumps her and departs for Harvard Law School, she chases after him, taking on aspects of the Claimant, the Amazon, and a slightly more sophisticated Temptress as she tries to win him back. But it's not until she realizes the futility of her quest—a realization prompted by the sneers of a clutch of Harvard Medusas—that she seriously begins to expand her range, not only deepening her roles as Claimant, Amazon, and Amiga but adding the Mesmerist to her repertoire as she bamboozles a friend's loutish ex, wins a coveted internship, saves a shy man from the withering gaze of two more Medusas, acquires a better love interest, and takes up a misunderstood client's cause. Throughout the middle of the film, she hides her Temptress under sober black suits and sensible shoes, but in the climactic courtroom sequence, she is once again a vision in hot pink and heels: fire, earth, water, and air united in one liberated, case-winning attorney. And in the very last scene, looking down on an adoring throng as she delivers the valedictory speech to her Harvard Law class, she is enthroned as the Empress.

Frozen: Inspired by Hans Christian Andersen's "The Snow Queen," *Frozen* features a woman who remains in one quadrant of the wheel (water-air) yet still grows large. Princess Elsa of Arendelle fears her primary archetype, which is, of course, the Snow Queen. Everything she touches turns to frost, especially when she's in the grip of emotion, so she's terrified of being

---

* I cite these films not because they are admirable in every way or free of patriarchal bias (they certainly aren't) but because they offer compelling examples of the archetypes in action.

touched—physically or emotionally—and locks herself away in a prison of her own making. She takes a step toward freedom when, after she is crowned and her powers are exposed, she becomes the Escapist: she runs away, isolating herself so she can stop suppressing her nature and "let it go" instead. But the archetypes of Snow Queen and Escapist are not enough to redeem her, for behind her she has left a snow-buried city with a freezing populace. In the end, with her sister Anna's help, she comes to realize that love is the answer: the force that will not only melt her ice fort of fear but also thaw her cold magic and harness it for good. In a flash of insight, she adopts the virtues of a third archetype, the Empath, thereby restoring family ties and turning her frozen capital into a winter wonderland.

Grease: As feminists we may roll our eyes at Sweet Sandy becoming Slut Sandy so she can get the guy, but let's admit: she was fabulous in those leather pants. With her scarlet lips, her teased-out hair, and her sultry "Tell me about it—*stud*," Olivia Newton-John creates a retina-searing image of a Temptress, an image rendered even sharper by its winking nod to the Jesteress and its contrast with the poodle-skirted Snow Queen, too prim and prissy for words, who came before. The movie's message, if we insist on finding one, is regressive; the imagery, however, is unforgettable, capturing a woman's ability to leap in the space of an afternoon from one archetype to its opposite, with the result that the world falls at her feet, electrified.*

The Help: In a small southern town in the 1960s, the Black women work as housekeepers and nannies for the white women. When first we meet Aibileen Clark she is pure Mama Bear, pouring all her excess maternal energy, deprived of its natural object by her son's death, into caring for her employer's little girl, who learns from Aibileen to repeat the mantra, "You is kind …you is smart…you is important." But Aibileen is also a storyteller, and

---

* I used to hate that Danny didn't have to change, too, until I realized he's the one who really *does* change, applying himself to the extent that he letters in track, while Sandy only adopts a new outfit and hairdo for, what—a few hours? I don't think she changes her nature; rather, she reveals her inner Temptress to bold effect.

when aspiring writer Skeeter Phelan is seeking content for a book about the lives of "the help," Aibileen agrees to share some of her stories. We see her start off in Mama Bear mode, talking of her son; then gradually, with the camera cutting back and forth from her to a wide-eyed Skeeter, we see her transform into the Mesmerist. The sight of a friend being arrested for petty theft at the behest of the town's most fearsome Medusa rouses Aibileen to become an Amazon, urging her peers to offer up their stories, too, for publication. She keeps her crusading hidden, however, even after the book comes out, and it's not until the Medusa lady threatens her with arrest that she finds the full Amazonian strength to confront her enemy head-on, blasting her with, "All you do is scare and lie to try to get what you want … You're a godless woman!" And then, tellingly: "Ain't you tired, Miss Hilly? Ain't you tired?" Only a Mama Bear, used to dealing with exhausted bratty kids, would put it quite that way.

13 Going on 30: This 2004 teen flick presents us with the case of a little Medusa girl who magically grows big—as in older—and learns a lesson about the limits of Medusa-dom. Jenna Rink, age thirteen, wants above all to be popular. To get in with the cool kids, she aims scorn at her best friend Matt, mocking him cruelly. But the cool kids serve her a nasty prank in return, and in her despair she makes a wish, inspired by a magazine article, to become "30, flirty, and thriving." With the aid of some pixie dust, her wish is granted. As 30-year-old Jenna, she discovers that she's a mean girl all grown up: a haughty magazine editor with a snarky best girlfriend, a dimwit boyfriend, a distant relationship with her parents, and no qualms about whom she destroys in her climb to the top. Her repertoire as an adult has, it seems, included many of the archetypes—Amiga, Temptress, Snow Queen, Jesteress, Claimant, Empress—but the worst aspects of each. It's only when she reencounters her old friend Matt that she begins to understand what she's lost in her pursuit of worldly success and, thus enlightened, to set about redeeming herself. She develops an Empath's compassion, acquires a true Amiga's sense of friendship, and with saving the magazine as her Amazonian cause, finally sheds her Medusa-girl meanness, growing big for real and for good.

A Couple of Concerns

"That's all very well," you might say, "but aren't these archetypes really just stereotypes? Worse, aren't they male-created stereotypes, based on dead men's dumb ideas about women?"

The answer to both questions is yes and no. Yes, archetypes can devolve into stereotypes, which in turn can be used to oppress. And yes, since most literature and art have been created by men and most religious practice has been controlled by men since civilization began, there's little doubt that each of the archetypes first took shape in a song, poem, or picture by a man and was perpetuated thereafter by male voices. Men have defined each archetype in relation to themselves: the Temptress seduces men, the Snow Queen rejects men, the Jesteress mocks men, the Witch destroys men, etcetera. Moreover, since I've chosen to use classic sources, you'll find that eleven of my twelve literary examples are from works by (or probably by) men, who were the vast majority of published authors until the mid-20th century. "We tend to see women through the eyes of men, which is a problem," says one feminist friend.

On the other hand, to quote feminist scholar Mary Daly, "We must smuggle back to other women our plundered treasures." Reclaimed as I intend, these archetypes don't degrade us; they lift us up. When we use them to understand our strengths, they help us play to those strengths. When we use them to see options we haven't seen, they serve as inspiration to do more and be more. The key is that *we're* the ones using them: reframing and applying them to our own ends.

As for the objection that stories written by long-dead men don't apply to us: that's based on the assumption that male bards only spout conventional dogma about women. This is not the case. The reason certain stories and characters last for centuries and span cultures is that they *transcend* the conventional views of their time and place. Take Homer's *Odyssey*: the portrait of Penelope (chapter 8), who fends off a horde of suitors vying to usurp the family estate in Odysseus's absence, is hardly that of a downtrodden housewife. Or consider Savitri (chapter 5), the Hindu princess who persuades Yama, the god of death, to return her husband; although modern storytellers have her "pleading" with Yama until he takes pity on her because she's such a faithful wife, the original Savitri is a masterful negotiator who, by aligning herself with the death god's interests—walking with him, literally and figuratively—leads him to the point where he wants to break his own law and do as she asks.

To understand the power of each archetypal woman, we must look to the best literary sources: not the ones that blither about sex kittens and mean mommies, but the ones featuring an expansive, even risky vision of what a woman can do and be.* Indeed the real danger of these archetypes isn't that they tie us to convention, but that they expose us to risks: most obviously with the fiery types who flout society's rules, less obviously with the other types—which makes their hazards all the greater. The Mesmerist weaves a spell that enchants her audience, but spells can go wrong and a disenchanted audience can turn ugly. The Empath with her gift for compassion is vulnerable to those who would take advantage of that gift. As for the Empress, you know the saying about the higher the rise, the farther the fall. (For ways to mitigate the risks, see Appendix: Do's and Don'ts for Each Archetype.)

Three Ways the Archetypes Empower Us

They help us appreciate our strengths. If you took the quiz at the start of this book, you already know the two or three archetypes where you're most at home. Knowing our home archetypes is one way to appreciate and build on our strengths. Typically, they'll be clustered in one area of the wheel. My own home types are in the airy northern zone: Escapist, Snow Queen, and Empress. It's good to know that the roles in which I naturally shine aren't mere personality tics, but potential sources of power and routes to success.

---

* Students of archetypes often look to fairy tales and myths, but I've focused mainly on classic literature. I love fairy tales, and I use one of the oldest ones as the basis for my concluding chapter; literary characters, however, tend to be more finely drawn, the situations they face more realistic, leading to richer insights in service of my goal: to "smuggle back" these archetypes, showing how they work for us today.

A friend and I still laugh about something he confessed to me once after a couple of drinks: "When I first met you," he said, "I thought you were uptight and unfriendly." He felt bad about letting that slip! But he was right: I *am* uptight and unfriendly. It's the Snow Queen in me—the introvert who stands aloof, relying on her frosty intellect to solve problems. When I think about it that way, I give myself permission to *be* myself. Like Elsa in *Frozen*, I can "let it go." *I am Snow Queen! Marvel at my ice palaces!*

They help us appreciate the strengths of other women. It's easy to observe someone acting in a way we wouldn't and dismiss her with a nasty epithet: "Skank." "Bitch." "Snob." When we keep the archetypes in mind, we can move past that initial, shallow reaction (a Medusa's reaction, by the way) to ask a better question: "Which archetype is she representing?" I don't mean to suggest we take women's goodness on faith; there are plenty of toxic women around, just as there are plenty of toxic men, and not all female behavior is well-intentioned. What I do suggest is that we give the woman whose behavior seems alien a second look and ask ourselves not what's wrong with her, but what we might learn from her.

Caroline, my former colleague whose story appears in chapter 1, was a classic Temptress, her fishnet stockings and flirtatious manner earning her more than a few side-eyes from the women at our company. Caroline went on to become a much-admired CEO, an award-winning entrepreneur, and a columnist for a major newspaper. I now realize I spent too much energy side-eyeing, not enough energy watching and learning.

They help us stretch beyond our comfort zone. Even if we find multiple archetypes congenial, there will always be some we find less so, and it's these, the ones we tend to suppress, that represent our opportunities for growth. Not that the leadership thinkers who tell us to play to our strengths are wrong; as I've said, it's no use trying to turn ourselves into something we're not. Playing to strengths, however, is a strategy more applicable to men than to women. Men, remember, can afford to be one-dimensional: they can set their sights on a goal, marshal their resources as tinker, tailor, soldier, or spy, and count on their unique skills to carry them through. James Bond never has to be Dirty Harry for the weekend. Samwell Tarly never has to be Jon Snow. We women, on the other hand, don't have the luxury to operate in one dimension. And why would we even try? Sure, we have particular talents and should make the most of them, but the real key to our success is our range, wider than any man's. For us, an expansion of repertoire holds more promise than reprisals of our greatest role.

And if we seek it, we'll likely find the "new" repertoire right there within us. I agree with Tony Binns, a freelance screenwriter who posted this on Facebook:

> The hero's journey fantasy for men is always starting at the bottom and coming into your own, so you are the complete badass at the end. The hero's journey fantasy for women is to be acknowledged for the power they already possess.

> This has real-world echoes. Men have been told to roll up shirt-sleeves and work their way to the top, whereas women are struggling to be heard, to not be interrupted, to be taken seriously, to not have their ideas stolen, and to have equal pay and opportunity as their male counterparts. Men fight for position; women fight for recognition.[2]

◆ ◆ ◆

Woman is born free, yet everywhere she is in chains: chains of discrimination, violence, abuse, limitation, trauma, self-doubt, self-absorption, fear, anger, shame.

The good news: by breaking big, we may break the chains.

There's a natural progression for women seeking personal or professional growth: a "developmental model," as my colleagues in the learning industry used to say. We start out attached to one or two archetypes, operating snugly in our comfort zone. When we find ourselves in situations where our favorite patterns don't work, we're apt to fall into the Medusa Trap, directing disdain toward men and even more toward other women. In this effort to puff ourselves up, we may reach for new models and, lacking a full understanding, latch onto their superficial aspects: the domineering Empress, the mocking Jesteress, the timid Escapist. These dress-up games only keep us small and weak, but when we grasp the deep truth of each archetype, reclaiming it from stereotype and building it up from within, we rise tall and mighty.

At the end of this book, having spent time with each archetype, we'll look to one of the world's oldest, most popular fairy tales for an example of a woman who masters the entire wheel of fire, earth, water, and air. When we can do the same, not because we have to but because we choose to, then we'll have accomplished our heroine's journey—and be insubordinate.

PART ONE

FIRE-EARTH

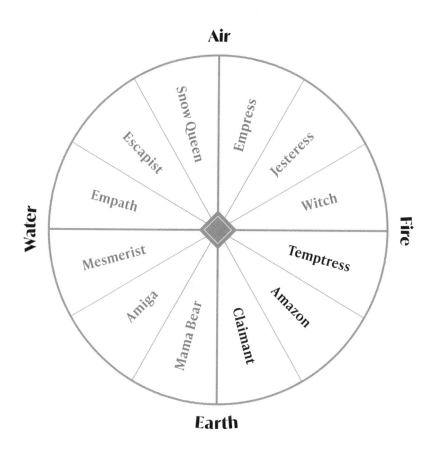

Air

Snow Queen

Empress

Escapist

Jesteress

Empath

Witch

Water

Fire

Mesmerist

Temptress

Amiga

Amazon

Mama Bear

Claimant

Earth

1

THE TEMPTRESS

"LOVE IS A REBELLIOUS BIRD that nobody can tame."[1]

So declares Carmen, cigar-roller at the tobacco factory in Seville. She and her coworkers have come outside on their break to enjoy the sunshine and flirt with the young men hanging around the plaza. The women lounge by the doorway, blowing cigarette smoke, their impudent glances and pursed lips drawing catcalls from all the men except one—Don José, an army corporal—who stands aside, head down, taking no notice of the scene. The rest of the fellows shout for *Carmen . . . Where is she? Where is Carmencita? Ah, there she is!* She saunters down the steps, laughing. The men crowd closer:

"Carmen, be kind . . . tell us on which day you'll love us!"[2]

To which she gaily replies, "When I'll love you? I've no idea!" And in her opening aria ("L'amour est un oiseau rebelle") we get the essence of the Temptress: the woman who not only accepts but revels in love's uncontrollability. "Love is a gipsy child," Carmen sings, "he has never known a law; though you don't love me, I love you, and if I love you, then beware!"[3]

Carmen: Wild at Heart

Carmen is one of the most popular operas ever composed, and for good reason. With a tempestuous score by Georges Bizet and a punchy libretto based on the novella of the same title by Prosper Mérimée, it has an erotic energy that captivates. I've listened to it many times; I've seen a stage production of *Carmen Jones*, Oscar Hammerstein's update, which uses Bizet's music but sets the action in a 1940s African American community; and I've seen several film versions of the story. Until my most recent listening, however, I failed to understand that the heroine's essential characteristic is not her overt sexiness (though she is sexy), but rather her **daring** in the arena of love. This daring is also the essence of the Temptress archetype.*

Right from the start Carmen says she's in love with love, not because love is comforting but because love is wild. Love comes and goes heedless of our wishes: turn away from it and it seizes you, demanding your attention; beg for it to attend you and it flies away, laughing. One man is handsome and charming, yet you find him a bore; another is plain and sullen, yet it's him you prefer. To Carmen, this unpredictability makes love not a miserable torment but a delightful game, a roller-coaster ride on which the aficionado lets go of the bar and screams to intensify the fun. Carmen's attitude is one of extreme openness, risking all for the thrill of being swept away. After her initial song she sees that among the men in the square, only Don José is ignoring her. This she finds intriguing, so as the factory bell clangs to recall the workers, she strolls over and tosses a flower casually at his feet. Thus she plays the part of rebellious love itself: *Here's a man who cares nothing for me. I choose him.*

Don José has the devotion of Micaela, a sweet, docile girl. In the next scene Micaela brings him a letter and a chaste kiss from his mother, indicating the old lady's wish that the two be married. But that tossed flower has Don José in a whirl, and when his superior officer sends him to detain Carmen for starting a fight on the factory floor, his fate is sealed. Far from

---

* My reading of Carmen as a character owes a lot to Camille Paglia's essay "Gypsy Tigress: Carmen," in *Vamps and Tramps* (New York: Vintage Books, 1994).

resisting arrest, Carmen uses the occasion to seduce the corporal, again not with sexy looks or moves but with offhand musings about the tavern she plans to visit with whoever agrees to be her new amour. There they will drink, they'll dance … "Who wants to love me? I'll love him. Who wants my heart? It's there for the taking."[4] *I have suitors by the dozen*, she says, *but I'll reject them all for—guess who? For you, Don José. Lawless love has chosen you.*

The poor man doesn't stand a chance. Sounding like a virginal girl hesitating in the arms of an importunate boyfriend, he begs Carmen to promise him: promise that, if he gives way, she'll love him, love him forever. "Yes," she says, "I'll love you." (She says nothing about forever.) He unties her hands and, when the officer returns to take her into custody, follows her lead in creating a ruckus that allows her to escape. He will serve a month in jail for it.

Act 2 showcases a second quality of the Temptress: her **gusto for life** and her ability to convey that gusto to others. The curtain rises on Carmen, a couple of her girlfriends, and some army officers gathered at a tavern near the city ramparts—that same tavern she sang of to Don José. Guitarists and drummers play. Bohemian girls dance. Carmen and her friends join in, throwing themselves with abandon into the "dazzling din … ardent, wild, feverish."[5] When the dance ends, Carmen learns from Lieutenant Zuniga that her lover is free as of this morning. She is delighted to hear it, but the next moment her attention is captured by a colorful parade in the street, which turns out to be in honor of the renowned bullfighter Escamillo. Lieutenant Zuniga invites the toreador to join their party, and when Escamillo sings of the excitement of the corrida—the shouts of the crowd, the rushes of the bull, and above all, the knowledge that "dark eyes are watching you, and that love awaits you"[6]—it's obvious that Carmen finds him fascinating: he's a kindred spirit, perhaps, and terribly handsome. Escamillo departs with promises to be thinking of her next time he slays a bull.

Still, Carmen remains entranced by thoughts of her simple corporal (remember, love is capricious), and when a couple of smuggler friends show up and beg the women to help them with a job, she says no. *Why not?* they ask. *I'm in love!* she replies. *So am I*, laughs one of the men, *but that doesn't mean I can't make myself useful.* Carmen laughs back, shaking her head: duty, money, usefulness, they are nothing compared to the glorious intoxication that is love. She knows Don José is coming to find her, and indeed, we hear his voice offstage. The smugglers leave with the other girls. Don José enters, and this dialogue ensues:

> *Carmen:* Here you are at last ... it's about time.

> *Don José:* It's only two hours since I left prison.

> *Carmen:* What stopped you leaving sooner? I sent you a file and a gold coin.

> *Don José:* But what then? I still have my honor as a soldier.[7]

He hands her the gold coin. Carmen can't believe it. He actually kept the coin instead of using it to bribe his way out, and is now returning it to her! In the soldier's upright gesture and the woman's stunned reaction we see the contrast I described earlier: men invest enormous meaning in rules and hierarchies, while women tend to find such scrupulosity, if not incomprehensible, faintly ridiculous. After all, if Don José was willing to break the law to help her escape, why was he so hung up on staying in jail for the prescribed time?

But no matter; now that she has the money back, Carmen will use it to good purpose. She calls for food and drink, lots of food and drink. *Let's eat everything, everything!* she says. She falls on the meal, gobbling the sweets like a child. Don José is once again enchanted. Carmen enjoys everything so much; he wants to have that passion in his own life. What he fails to see is that he can't have Carmen's passion without Carmen's willingness to be overcome, to lose control for the sake of the ecstasy that losing control imparts. When she tells him she danced in front of Lieutenant Zuniga, he grows angry. *Are you jealous?* she asks. *Of course I'm jealous*, he replies. She offers to dance for him, for him alone, but he's only partly mollified. He wants to own her, as a conventional husband owns a conventional wife. We, the audience, understand what Don José does not and never will: if he could own Carmen, she wouldn't be Carmen, and the wild passion he seeks would elude him.

Besides her romantic daring and her appetite for life's pleasures, Carmen exemplifies a third quality of the Temptress: **defiance of authority**. We've seen this quality already, when in act 1 Zuniga arrested her for fighting and she sang, "Tra la la la … cut me up, burn me, I'll tell you nothing, tra la la. I defy everything–fire, steel, and heaven itself!"[8] In acts 3 and 4 she continues to reject all rules in the name of liberty, glorious liberty. "Give me liberty or give me death," said Patrick Henry; Carmen would have recognized the American revolutionary as a brother, for she is equally sure about her preference for death over a life constrained.

After a jealous Don José runs afoul of the law yet again by attacking the lieutenant (who returned to the tavern with a dalliance in mind), he has no choice but to join the smugglers, their girlfriends, and Carmen as they all head for the mountains. The group spends some weeks as bandits roving town to town. Carmen is in her element: the wide world her country, her wish the law. But she's already sick of Don José–we can imagine what a wet blanket he must be, whining about the cold, worrying they'll get caught–and when he asks her to make peace, she tells him bluntly: "No, what I want is to be free and to do what I like."[9] She drops more scorn on him when they take a rest high above a valley and he waxes maudlin about the dear old lady, his mother, who lives down there. *Dear old lady?* Carmen scoffs. He dares her to say it again. She shakes with laughter: *Then what, you'll kill me?* When he calls her a devil, she only laughs harder: *Of course! I told you I was.*

Don José has another violent encounter, this time with Escamillo, the toreador, who after the scuffle walks away proclaiming his greater interest in fighting bulls than fighting jealous boyfriends. A bit later Micaela shows up again, come to tell Don José his mother wants to see him. Carmen informs Don José flat out that if he runs off to visit mama, she's done with him. Then Micaela reveals the sad news: his mother is dying. It's too much for Don José. He tells Carmen he's going home but will be back soon. Carmen shrugs.

The final act takes place a week or two later, outside the bullring in Seville.

Food vendors are hawking their wares, children are running about, and an excited crowd is flooding in the gate. Enter a parade of picadors, banderilleros, and finally Escamillo himself—with Carmen, resplendent in a golden dress and gold jewelry, on his arm. Carmen's girlfriend hurries over and whispers to her to beware, for Don José is somewhere near, and he's angry. Carmen says she's not afraid. She stays behind as Escamillo and retinue pass into the ring.

Soon enough, Don José appears and begs Carmen to come back to him. No, she says, she will do as she pleases, and yes, yes, Escamillo is her new lover—she'll declare her love for him in the face of death itself! "Never will Carmen give in. Free she was born and free she will die."[10] Don José pleads, to no avail. He threatens, to no avail. Finally he draws a dagger and blocks Carmen's path:

> *Don José:* No, by my blood, you shall not go. Carmen, it's with me you're coming!

> *Carmen:* No, no! Never!

> *Don José:* I'm tired of threatening.

> *Carmen:* Well then, stab me, or let me pass.

> *Don José:* For the last time, you devil, will you come with me?[11]

She will not. She rips his ring from her finger and throws it at him with a shriek of rage. He stabs her. She falls dead. With the roar of the bullring crowd as backdrop, the onetime soldier sinks to his knees, crying: "You can arrest me. I killed her. Carmen! My adored Carmen!"

She went out on her own terms, risking everything for the wild joys of love.

Caroline: Fishnets and Flowers

Of all the archetypes the Temptress is the one most likely to be seen through male eyes, so we must work hard to reclaim her as a role model, rejecting the caricatures shaped by men and making a study of her true qualities— which, we may be surprised to find, are transferable from opera stage to office cubicle. Of course what we see in opera is art, not reality; no one is saying we have to be stabbed by our ex-lover in front of a bullring in order to earn our Temptress card.* Let's examine this archetype further and see how it applies to our everyday lives.

The Temptress is not a sex toy or a whore. She is not a dominatrix in thigh-high boots or a sugar-baby in a pushup bra. Indeed, the Temptress wears whatever she likes—though she won't hesitate to flaunt her physical assets, if doing so will help her attract the type of attention she wants from whom she wants. Her main characteristic, as I've said, is her daring: not only in matters of erotic love but in the whole sphere of personal relationships. We might call her a daredevil of human connection.

Such a daredevil was Caroline, a marketing executive at the consulting firm where I worked beginning in 1989. Caroline had lustrous dark hair, a wide smile, and an infectious laugh. She had nice legs, which from time to time she would encase in fishnet hose. (While nylons or tights were standard professional wear for women back then, fishnets certainly were not.) A Harvard Business School alumna, she was acknowledged by all to be a brilliant mind and was never shy about taking credit for successes. One of my first memories of her

---

* It's impossible to see or listen to *Carmen* without thinking about the psychology of intimate-partner violence. Don José is the quintessence of the male domestic abuser: control is his motivation, though he claims to be driven by love. Because he can't bear Carmen's rejection, he kills her, thereby becoming a literary instance of an all-too-real multitude of murderous men spanning the globe and stretching back through the ages, whose wives and girlfriends died at their hands. But that's a book-length topic in itself, so I'll just note here, lest anyone worry that Don José's actions are being romanticized, that Carmen is the clear protagonist of the piece. She is strong, Don José is weak. She is aware, he is deluded. She has nobility, he has none. While there surely is romance in the work, it is all due to Carmen and her unshakeable determination to live life as she will.

occurred a few weeks after I'd started at the company, at an all-staff gathering in the lobby of our Boston headquarters. Our CEO was running through the results for the quarter, and when he announced the goal-beating rollout of a new product, Caroline yelled out: "That one's mine!" Nothing about *my team* or *ours*—just *mine*. Pretty self-centered, right? But her tone was so happy, so unselfconsciously exuberant, that the braggadocio didn't seem to matter.

Caroline's daredevil nature showed up in numerous ways. She relished pushing boundaries and having them pushed by others. I remember the time I attended an internal training session that she was leading; this was back in the days of flipcharts as visual aids—no PowerPoint—and she was up at the easel making her presentation when suddenly (or so it seemed) she recalled a funny story. A few years back, she told us, she had been leading a similar session in that very same conference room. She had been giving her usual spiel, turning the flipchart sheets without looking at them, when all at once every mouth in the audience fell open. "What?" she asked. People pointed at the easel. She turned to look, and—oh my!—pasted on the sheet was a large, seminude magazine photo. A couple of her colleagues had stuck it there as a prank. I recall how, as she told this story, she mimed her own shock, leaning back and throwing up her hands with fingers splayed. "What a riot!" she said, chortling. "They really got me!" We all laughed along.

Just as often, she was the prankster. She was always one of the stars of the company's annual stage show, the Follies, not only leading and writing lyrics for a spoofy acapella quintet called The Five Whys, but also appearing in skits that sometimes pushed the limits, shall we say, of corporate decorum.

It was a different era, of course; today, most shenanigans like that are out of bounds, and rightly so. But even back then, it was interesting: although there were plenty of eye-rolls and the occasional catty comment about Caroline's over-the-top behavior, she was universally respected, even loved, by her team, her clients, and really everyone in her orbit. "The way she acted was unorthodox sometimes," said a colleague of mine, "but I never felt manipulated or put down. She made you feel like she really cared about you. Some people are all about results, but I felt she led with relationships. She used relationship energy to get results."

Relationship energy. It's a perfect term for the Temptress's main tool, which she wields intentionally (or perhaps instinctually), directing it as a spotlight on this person and that. A star, they say, is someone who makes you feel as if he or she is performing for you alone—just you, among hundreds in the theater—and Caroline had that star quality. When she shone her spotlight on you it felt good, if a little unsettling. She was the original close-talker: she would invade your personal space, putting a hand on your back or shoulder. She would hold eye contact a few seconds longer than appropriate. She would nod and smile as if you were the most fascinating person she'd ever met. All of this gave you the sense you were special; that, like Corporal Don José, you had been chosen by somebody exciting, somebody big.

Though Caroline's attitude could have a sexual buzz, it didn't always. In 2010, some twelve years after she had left to start her own firm, I ran into her again. I had recently coauthored my first leadership book, and I'd been invited along with a couple of other authors to give a talk to the Harvard Business School Alumni Association. Caroline was chairing the panel discussion that followed. We hadn't seen each other in all that time, and I didn't expect her to take notice of me beyond what would be expected for professional courtesy; she was now a successful CEO, on the verge of selling the firm she'd founded, and in any case our paths hadn't crossed much back in the day. But when the event was over and we speakers were mingling with the guests, I got cornered by a very persistent woman who wanted to tell me all about her job search. I'd been standing there for ten minutes as the woman talked on about her qualifications, and I guess I was looking a bit desperate, for suddenly I felt someone at my side. It was Caroline.

"I'm *so* sorry," she said, beaming at the job hunter, "I just have to introduce Jocelyn to *mumble-mumble.*" She tucked her arm through mine and led me away. After a few steps she leaned in even closer and whispered in conspiratorial fashion, "I'm saving you."

And boy, I felt saved. Not only that, but I felt I had a new best friend. Like Carmen with Don José, Caroline had tossed the flower at my feet, singling me out for attention. If she was merely amusing herself, I didn't care. I'd received plenty of applause for my speech, but applause couldn't compare to her arm linked with mine as she took me off, whispering gleefully in my ear.

Our stint as besties didn't last long. We walked around the room together for a bit, chatting of this and that. She introduced me to a few people, talking me up as "brilliant, such an expert, have you read her book?" Then she had to go, and she pressed her card on me as she told me to call her "any time! We'll have drinks!" I knew I'd never call, no more than she would. The Temptress is a creature of the moment; her spotlight shines and moves on. But while you're in that light, you feel special. Are you her best friend, her crush, a member of her secret club? It doesn't matter. You're *in*. And you know it's going to be mad fun.

Learning from the Temptress

How can we incorporate the wild ways of the Temptress into our own (no doubt less wild) work and personal lives? Here are three lessons to take from Carmen and Caroline.

Make people feel special. According to poet Maya Angelou, "People will forget what you did, they'll forget what you said, but they'll never forget how you made them feel." The Temptress is able to make people *feel* good, and she uses that ability to tremendous effect. Most of us tend to underestimate our power in this regard. "Why should anyone care if I pay attention to them?" we wonder. "After all, I'm nobody important." We go through each day waiting for someone to shine a spotlight on *us*, forgetting that we, too, carry a spotlight and can shine it on whomever we choose. We forget that every human being, from the summer intern to the CEO, wants that glow: wants to feel noticed, appreciated, liked. Obviously our attentions must not cross the line (as Caroline's arguably did sometimes), but there are myriad small, harmless ways to make someone feel like a star. Here are just a few:

Smile and say, "How are you today?" Ask about their family. Listen intently when they speak. Say, "I agree with you," then amplify their point. Ask them about their preferences, how they like to work. Remember something they said a week ago. Talk up their achievements. Say, "That was excellent work you did." Say, "I love your shoes." Say, "Thank you."

The list goes on. A male Temptress I knew, the head of a regional office, used to refer to me now and then as "the Great Jocelyn Davis." It wasn't just me; he did it with everyone. But it never seemed insincere, and I must say, it endeared him to me. It made me feel special.

Bring the fun. Nobody likes a Debbie Downer. Maybe you or I couldn't laugh at the sort of risqué prank Caroline had played on her, and maybe we shouldn't have to; nevertheless, outside of campaigns of real intimidation or sexual harassment, it's usually best to chuckle along with jokes made at our expense. Even outright insults are best shrugged off with a grin. Think of Carmen's reaction when Don José calls her a devil: *Of course! I told you I was!*

More important, you want to be the person who, when she walks in a room, makes everyone think, "Oh good, she's here!" rather than "Oh. *She's* here." If you're an introvert like me, you might worry about this advice because you know you'll never be the life of the party. But it's not about creating a party; it's about creating a sense of enjoyment, of energy and lightness. This means being the person who laughs at someone's funny story and supports someone else's slightly off-the-wall idea. It means being the person who shows up for meetings on time, with a nod and a friendly word for everyone, and sits at the table looking interested—rather than the person who slinks in late, spends five minutes glumly inspecting the muffin tray, then slumps in a far corner slurping her coffee (which, by the way, has been me too many times). It means being the manager who brings donuts, or remembers her staff's birthdays, or inserts a couple of silly activities into an offsite as relief from the PowerPoint marathon. Most of all, it means being quick to smile and slow to take offense.

Let them see you like them. Whether in social or professional contexts, we often hide our fondness for others. Perhaps it's because we don't want to appear vulnerable; perhaps it's because we want to maintain the upper hand in a competitive situation. As we saw with Carmen, however, there can be great power in *showing* our predilection. Carmen's open stroll across the square to Don José and the flower she so blatantly tosses at his feet make her irresistible to him. "It's really obvious when you like someone," said a guy I knew back in college. I was chagrined, until he added, "It's very attractive."

The key is to avoid an air of desperation. There's a huge difference between the person who seems to need you in order to make their life tolerable and the person who seems to have everything they need already and would simply love for you to join the fun. *There's this tavern*, says Carmen to her choice of man. *All my friends go there. We have a blast, and I want you to come with me.* We can take that same inviting attitude with potential friends, customers, or anyone we want to be closer to. The Temptress knows it's not the woman playing hard to get who is most enticing, but the woman laying her cards on the table—cards that say, *I like you. I bet you like me, too.*

◆ **2** ◆

THE AMAZON

"LET THE MEN COME; they won't bother me. They can threaten what they like—even try to set fire to the place—they won't make us open the gates except on our own terms."[1]

Respectable Greek matron Lysistrata is leading a sex strike. Until the men of Athens, Sparta, and their respective allies agree to stop a war that has dragged on for decades, the women of those city-states—young and old, rich and poor, wives and prostitutes—will be locking it down (so to speak). Lysistrata has her crew of conspirators repeat this oath:

> I will not allow either lover or husband to approach me in a state of erection. And I will live at home in unsullied chastity, wearing my saffron gown and my sexiest makeup, to inflame my husband's ardor. But I will never willingly yield myself to him.[2]

With that, they retire into the Acropolis and bar the gate. "Before long," says their fearless leader, "we will be known throughout Greece as the Liquidators of War."

Lysistrata: Anti-war Warrior

When playwright Aristophanes presented his comedy *Lysistrata* at Athens's annual drama festival in 411 BCE, the Peloponnesian War had been raging for 20 years. Two years earlier, the city's navy had been nearly destroyed in an expedition against Sicily, leaving Athens wide open to the Spartan forces pressing them on land and sea and to the attacks of former vassal states that had seized the opportunity to switch sides. By 411, things were looking up a bit: Athens had rebuilt the navy using a reserve fund set aside at the war's start and stored in temples on the Acropolis, and the great general Alcibiades, exiled from both Athens and Sparta, was sending messages from afar promising to bring the Persians into the conflict as Athenian allies. Still, the Spartan army wasn't flagging. To the average Athenian, the war would have seemed an ordeal with no way out.[3]

In Aristophanes's play, however, there *is* a way out—thanks to the bold vision of Lysistrata, who on a bright summer morning calls together not only her Athenian friends but also (suspend your disbelief; this is a comedy) female representatives of Sparta, Corinth, Thebes, and many other Greek cities. When questioned as to her purpose, Lysistrata throws a question back at the ladies gathered before her: "The fathers of your children—don't you miss them when they're away at the war? I know that not one of you has a husband at home."[4]

They all agree the situation is dire. For months, there's been hardly a man in the city. Thanks to trade disruptions, even the supply of leather dildos has been cut off! Lysistrata presses on: "Well then, if I found a way to do it, would you be prepared to join with me in putting a stop to the war?"[5] *Yes!* cry all the women. *We'll do anything! We'll give our lives if need be!*

"Then I will tell you my plan," says Lysistrata. "Women, if we want to force the men to make peace, we must renounce . . ." She hesitates. ". . . sex."

Horrified refusals ensue. *Renounce sex? Never!* Several of the company are on the point of leaving, but Lysistrata persists, laying out her scheme and eventually persuading them all to her side. Under her direction, the old women of the city have already commandeered Athena's temple on the Acropolis with its stores of gold. And by the end—after much action involving water fights, screaming matches, stripping of clothes, and men hopping about the stage with painfully large erections–the women have won, and peace reigns across Greece.

All farce, of course, and you might wonder why I've chosen such a funny play as setting for the Amazon, who fights as easily as she breathes. It's because Lysistrata and her female army, though pursuing a goal of peace, personify this most warlike of the archetypes in three ways: (1) they make no compromise, (2) they show no fear, and (3) they have no self-doubt.

Upon hearing Lysistrata's proposal, the women come up with all sorts of excuses and objections. How can anyone give up sex? It'll be much too … hard. And what if one's husband drags one into the bedroom? What if he resorts to force, as seems likely? Lysistrata will brook **no compromise**. "Make yourself frigid … Make life a misery for them, and they'll give up trying soon enough," she says grimly.[6] She has the group take an oath, a real oath over a cup of blood-red wine, that no matter how desperate they grow they will not willingly sleep with husband, lover, or any man until peace is achieved. Days later, when some of the ladies start inventing fanciful reasons for deserting the cause–one claims she has to go home and spread her fleeces on the bed lest they get moths–Lysistrata holds them to their vow:

Lysistrata: You're not spreading anything on any bed, and you're not going anywhere.

Woman: And I'm to leave my fleeces to be ruined?

Lysistrata: If necessary, yes.[7]

Interesting that in the opening scene, it is Lampito, the Spartan lady–that is, the representative of Athens's principle enemy–who is first to sign onto the plan. But then Spartans were famous for their stern discipline and indifference to comfort (hence our adjective *spartan*), so perhaps it's not so strange. Lampito admits that going without sex will be a sore trial, "but still I'll say aye, for we must have peace." Lysistrata embraces her, crying,

"Oh, Lampito darling, you're the only *real* woman here!"[8] A real woman, it seems, is a woman who doesn't waffle.

Soon after the women have commandeered the temple, a bevy of old men arrives with logs, torches, and coal pots. They proclaim their intent to burn out the rebels and set about trying to light the walls on fire, without much success. From the opposite direction a band of old women approaches carrying bowls and jugs of water, the **fearless** Stratyllis at their head. Right away Stratyllis begins to hurl invective at the unnamed Men's Leader: "What have we got here? A gang of male scum, that's what! No man who had any decency, or respect for the gods, would behave like this!" The Men's Leader expresses astonishment at this swarm of female belligerents. "What are you so frightened for?" Stratyllis jeers. "Are there that many of us?" The Men's Leader raises his fist and threatens to shut her up, but Stratyllis merely presents her cheek: "All right, there you are, hit me. I won't shy away. Only, if you do, no *other* bitch will ever grab your bollocks again!" He threatens to bash her with *both* fists; what will she do then, eh? "I'll tear out your lungs and guts with my teeth!" she yells.[9]

Suffice to say, Stratyllis is up for a fight. Upon reading her stream of ferocious abuse—there's a lot more of it—all I could think was that here we have the ultimate angry feminist of men's nightmares: the creature whose demands for justice sound, to male ears, like nothing but shrewish vilification. ("You just hate men!" cried the guys in one contentious Facebook group I used to frequent, whenever someone ventured the radical opinion that women are humans with human rights; it never failed to send them into a tizzy.) Yes, Stratyllis does seem enraged, but why shouldn't she be? The men are setting fire to the most sacred site in the city. And every insult she flings is in direct response to a threat by her adversary:

Men's Leader: What have you brought water here for, you goddamned scum?

Stratyllis: Well, how about you, you old corpse? What's that torch for? Your funeral pyre?

Men's Leader: No—for your friends in there, for *their* funeral pyre.

Stratyllis: And we've got the water here to put your pyre out!

Men's Leader: Put our pyre out? . . . I'm just wondering whether to give you a light roasting right away.

Stratyllis: If you've got some soap, I'll be happy to give you a bath![10]

With that, she orders her crone battalion to advance with their jugs of water, and soon they have the men's side shivering like a passel of drowned rats. Liquidators of War, these ladies are.

Few things seem to disconcert a man more than a woman who won't be cowed. For the Men's Leader, clearly used to females who sweetly concede a point, a gang of women punching back is shocking. Aristophanes, I think, knew he could count on the men in his audience to feel that same sense of shock, and he plays it for laughs. Perhaps he realized that comedy is one of the few ways men can relate to an Amazon: a real Amazon, that is, not a male-fantasy Amazon in Wonder Woman hot-pants.

Equally disconcerting is the women's **lack of self-doubt**. When the city magistrate shows up at the Acropolis—it's now some weeks into the sex strike, and the men are feeling the pain—Lysistrata emerges to confront him. What follows is the *agon*, the literal meaning of which is "conflict" but in Greek drama was the term for a formal debate on the crucial issues of the play.

The magistrate begins by asking Lysistrata what she means by shutting and barring the temple against them. "We want," she replies, "to keep the money safe and stop you from waging war." The women will take charge of the treasury from now on. The magistrate is astounded: *women*, in charge of state funds? Lysistrata says wives have always managed the household finances, so what's the big deal?

Magistrate: But that's not the same thing.

Lysistrata: Why not?

Magistrate: Because the money here is needed for the war!

Lysistrata: Ah, but you shouldn't be *at* war.

Magistrate: How else can we keep the City safe?

Lysistrata: We'll see it's kept safe.

Magistrate: You!!!

Lysistrata: Us.

Magistrate: This is intolerable!

Lysistrata: We're going to save you, whether you like it or not.[11]

The magistrate sputters on, alternating between outrage at Lysistrata's thinking she can *save* him and befuddlement that a woman is taking an interest in matters of war and peace. With relentless calm, Lysistrata explains that for ages the women of Athens have been enduring whatever the men did, smiling and staying quiet in the face of major political blunders. "But don't think we approved!" she says. After watching their husbands make one stupid decision after another, the women have finally decided to unite and save Greece. "You listen to us," says Lysistrata, "listen to us and keep quiet, like you made us do, and we'll set you to rights."[12]

What's most striking to me about this exchange—and the rest of the agon, in which she enumerates the harms caused by the war and expounds her theory of political leadership—is Lysistrata's absolute certainty that she and, by implication, all the women *know what's right*. Moreover, they've known it all along; they just haven't chosen to take a stand until now. Is her self-assurance genuine or merely a show? It hardly matters. In the end, when the men are brought to heel and Lysistrata stands between the Athenian and Spartan delegations, leading the peace negotiations, we know she triumphed largely because her front had zero cracks. Not for her the claim of Socrates to know nothing; *she knows*, and she'll not back down.

No compromise, no fear, and no self-doubt: with these three lacks, the Amazon makes men throw up their hands and conclude, in the words of the hapless Men's Leader: "There is no beast more stubborn than a woman, and neither fire nor leopard is more ruthless."[13]

Lacey: Consultative Selling Be Damned

One of the project managers at our firm in the 1990s was an Amazon named Lacey.

Lacey was short and solid with bobbed brown hair, a forthright gaze through wire-rimmed glasses, and a fast walk. I, as a junior editor, was terrified of her. She would materialize at my cubicle doorway at eight thirty a.m., bark, "How are you?!" and proceed to announce, rapid fire, that she had a massive project on deck for Important Client X to be handed off tomorrow and which needed an ultra-fast turnaround so I might want to summon extra help and what other information did I need right now? "Nothing," I'd squeak. "Great, see you tomorrow," she'd snap—and off she'd motor. One thing I liked about her was that she always followed process, dutifully filling out whatever forms were required and organizing her handoffs clearly; woe unto anyone, though, who missed a deadline or made a mistake on one of her projects. Her nickname around the office was The Pit Bull.

Over the next few years I grew less intimidated by Lacey, partly because when she moved into a role as a department manager I saw her less often, but also because I began to appreciate her for her most notable quality: directness. Our company culture was extremely "nice," which had its advantages but also its drawbacks, one of which was that you could never be quite sure whether someone who was all niceness to your face was trashing you behind your back. (Watch out for those Medusas!) But Lacey, if she had a problem with you, would come right out and say it. I liked that, and so did many others. Her team members, while acknowledging she could lack grace, sang her praises as a manager. I must have heard it a dozen times: "With Lacey, you always know where you stand."

Her directness marked her as an Amazon from the start, but her Amazonian success didn't emerge fully until she decided to leave and start her own company. She was a single mother, and the market was competitive. It cannot have been easy. I remember I ran into her long about 2001, a few years into her solo venture. I asked her how business was.

"Great," she said. "I've got more than I can handle."

"What's your secret?" I asked.

"I take all work," she said. "You know, when I announced I was leaving, my boss was very supportive and asked me, 'So, Lacey, what type of projects are you looking for? What are your goals? What do you *want*?' And I was like, 'I want to feed my child.'" She shrugged. "That's what I want. So I don't turn anything down."

A dozen years later I, too, went out on my own. Lacey, who by that time had a stable of independent contractors working for her, was the first to call me up. Over the next few years I joined her on several projects, and I can report that it was a consistent pleasure. Her habit was to make her expectations clear, lay out the rules, and leave you alone to get on with your piece. If she was disappointed in something, she let you know; if she was pleased, likewise, she let you know. The total lack of bullshit was refreshing. Plus, she paid well. It did not surprise me that her contractors praised her as loudly as her team members used to do.

What did surprise me, somewhat, was her success with clients.

For context, here's a little background on the sales philosophy that has long prevailed in the corporate world. It's called *consultative selling*. The consultative salesperson's role is never to push or persuade, indeed never to "sell," but rather to help the customer make a wise decision. Consultative salespeople do not talk about their products; they explore needs. They do not pitch solutions; they let the customer choose the best solution for herself. They do not close transactions; they build relationships. The top three skills of consultative selling are listening, questioning, and confirming. If you think it sounds like psychological counseling, you're not far wrong; although the focus is business problems, not personal problems, a consultative salesperson is supposed to be just as diffident about providing answers, just as adept at guiding clients toward their own answers, as any shrink. Since the early 1970s, consultative selling has been business dogma. If you don't practice it, say the salesforce experts, you may enjoy short-term gains, but ultimately your customers will abandon you and your business will wither.

Lacey made no fetish of consultative selling. "In fact," said one colleague, "she can be the opposite of consultative. In many sales situations she's pound-pound-pound. She's advocating; she's prescriptive. She's all about results first, relationships second."

Yet her loyal clients multiplied and her business thrived. Why? My friend explained:

> She comes across as a real expert. She has a ton of stories to share: "We tried that at Company A, and it didn't work. We did this other thing at Company B, and it worked great. So here's what you should do." Clients seem to like that. They trust her. They know at the end of the day, she'll get it done.

I had a firsthand view of Lacey's non-consultative selling method when she hired me to help her design a training program for a California-based consumer products company. Our client, Kathy, was new to her role as training director and faced a beast of a task: corralling dozens of different stakeholders, none of whom agreed on what needed to happen, plus managing a difficult longtime employee who had been working on the program for eighteen months with very little to show for it and was damned if anyone was going to tread on his turf. Kathy, who had worked with Lacey before, was open about the desperation she felt. "I can't do this on my own," she said. "I need the cavalry." (She might have said, "I need an Amazon.")

Lacey rode to the rescue. With her trademark directness, she came across in every meeting as utterly assured. Rather than explore options—one of the core techniques of consultative selling—she made recommendations, and she encouraged me to do the same. Not that we were inflexible; if Kathy demurred, we'd listen and adapt. But when Kathy's difficult employee started advocating for still-more-thorough needs assessments and demanding we use his original plan for the program, Lacey cut him off with, "We're not doing that." After a few weeks the employee went on leave, claiming the stress we were causing him was too much. Kathy, I suspect, was secretly pleased. And in the end, the program was a hit.

Now, not all clients are in Kathy's situation; some do need a soft-voiced counselor rather than a hard-charging knight in armor. And the "here's what you should do" approach only works if you truly have the expertise to back it up. But Lacey knew that when a client pays good money for your services, nine times out of ten they aren't paying you to stand around making encouraging noises; they're paying you to solve a problem, a problem they can't solve on their own. They are paying you, in effect, to save them. And if you encounter a difficult person who, like the Magistrate in *Lysistrata*, does not want to be saved, well . . . as the Amazon, you go ahead and save him anyway.

Learning from the Amazon

Here are four lessons we can take from happy warriors Lysistrata and Lacey.

Know what you want. As women we're not used to thinking about, let alone stating, what we want. In times of conflict we're inclined, rather, to ruminate on blame: *Is it my fault? Is it his fault? Why is he being such a jerk? How can I make him see what a jerk he is?* Rarely do we shut off the blame-o-meter and turn our considerable intelligence to the plain question: *What do I want in this situation?* And even if we do ask that question, our answers are often nebulous: *I want to be happy. I want him to be nicer. I want everything to be better.* Not good enough; not for an Amazon. The Amazon knows exactly what she wants.

Lysistrata knew exactly what she wanted when she initiated the sex strike: to bring an end to the war. Lacey knew exactly what she wanted when she started her company: to make enough money to support her child. It sounds ridiculously obvious, but to get what you want, you must know what it is you want. Otherwise, you'll be galloping blind.

Find allies. Notice that the first thing Lysistrata does isn't to rush off to the Acropolis and make a stirring speech about the evils of war, but rather to call together women from a number of Greek cities, including Athens's chief enemy, and persuade them to join her effort. Only once these allies are on board does she make her move.

Too often, we women imagine that the apparent justice of our cause will be enough. "When I raise my banner," we think, "everyone will flock to it." So we spend days polishing and rehearsing our presentation, staking all on our performance in the big meeting. Men know better. They know the most important meeting is actually the pre-meeting—or pre-*meetings*, plural—in which they gain buy-in to their plan, one colleague at a time. If you would be an Amazon, follow the men's example: well before making your first foray, line up your allies.

Be sure in your rightness. "Here lies the body of William Jay, who died maintaining his right of way. He was right, dead right, as he sped along; now he's just as dead as if he'd been wrong."[14] I love that old bit of doggerel and have used it often to illustrate my view that our efforts to be right should never outstrip our efforts to be effective, that we should always be ready to slow down or change course. Upon reflection, however, I think it's mostly men who should heed that advice about flexibility; women, not so much.

Whether because of nature or nurture, we women have a tendency to doubt ourselves—witness the fact that there are many more William Jays lead-footing it down the road of life than there are Wilhelmina Jays. Speaking for myself, I can't recall a time when I approached a conflict with absolute assurance I was right, yet it's ironic: in the one or two big professional battles I've engaged in, my male adversary was quick to accuse me of self-righteousness. "Have you ever *once* considered you might be wrong?" fumed one guy in an email. It's almost as if men know we're afraid of seeming overconfident and that they can turn that fear as a weapon against us.

I propose we stop handing them the weapon. Of course most of the time we'll want to avoid brawls, but on those occasions when we've committed to one—committed with specific and good intent, as I discuss below—it serves no purpose to start doubting ourselves halfway through. Better to stick to our guns and repeat after old Stratyllis: "My gender has no bearing on the question / Whether I'm offering you a good suggestion."[15]

Fight with good intent. The Amazon has a reputation for being an indiscriminate scrapper, charging into any and all frays with a bloodthirsty yell; in my two examples of this archetype, however, I see as much discernment as ferocity. Lysistrata has thought deeply about the harm being done by the war, the benefits to be gained from peace, and the type of government she wishes to promote after peace is made. My real-life colleague Lacey never recommended a plan to a client without experience and evidence to say it was the best plan for them. A true Amazon does not lash out at random. She picks her battles. Moreover, though it may look like she's fighting *with someone*, she's really fighting *for something*, and she sincerely believes the *something* is in her adversary's best interest. In the words of deceased US congressman John Lewis, an Amazon gets into "good trouble."

I remember the time I confronted my elderly mother about her excessive drinking. In the lead-up to this mini-intervention, my adrenaline was surging as if I were about to have a physical fight. Expecting an angry reaction, I had braced myself for battle—but no battle came. Although my mom seemed a little bewildered at first, she remained calm, listened, asked a few questions, then stated her resolve to change. And change she did. The intervention worked.

To this day I remain surprised. I cannot put my success down to eloquence, for I remember stumbling over my words, forgetting all the fine arguments I had marshaled for the agon. Nor do I think it was my force of will that won the day. I think, rather, it was my bedrock good intent; a concern not for my own well-being (I lived far away, and it wasn't much skin off my nose if she drank) but for hers, and my father's. Somehow I managed to convey that concern, and she responded to it.

A happy warrior is the last thing I am. That one time, though, I managed to call up the spirit of the Amazons: the women who war in good cause.

3

THE CLAIMANT

"**THIS IS YOUR SON, SIRE** ... Now act with him as you promised, greatest of men."[1]

Shakuntala and her son have come to the court of Hastinapura, ancient City of Elephants and royal seat of India. The boy is the king's, conceived six years ago. Roaming through the forest on a hunting trip, King Dushanta had spied Shakuntala, beautiful foster daughter of an ashram-dwelling sage, and within a matter of days had fallen in love (or was it only lust?) and taken her hand in marriage. When he returned to court, he left his young, pregnant wife behind with a promise that her child would, in time, be named his heir. "I will conduct you to my city, sweet-smiling woman, as you deserve," he said back then. "This I declare to you as my truth, my lovely."[2] Shakuntala made him swear to it. Now, she has brought her son to the capital and is asking that he be recognized.

Her hands are on the boy's shoulders, her stance erect. "Remember the promise you made long ago when we lay together, man of fortune," she says. The courtiers' heads swivel to her, then to the throne. After a long pause, the king speaks:

"I do not remember."

Shakuntala: A Righteous Claim

When we think female archetypes, the Claimant probably isn't one that pops to mind. This ancient type, though she appears often in old folklore and literature, has lain relatively quiet for the past century—perhaps because her claims were typically founded on her status as a wife and mother, roles that as an unintended consequence of the women's movement have, in recent decades, lost some of their traditional force. I do not say that women should be shoved back into the wife-mother box; not at all. What I do say is that the Claimant, a.k.a. the Woman with a Righteous Demand, is due for another look, for she holds forgotten power upon which we all might draw. On the archetypes wheel she sits between Amazon and Mama Bear, earthier than the former, more blazing than the latter, and differing from the Amazon mainly in her stillness: while the Amazon charges into battle, sword raised high, the Claimant plants her feet on the ground, saying, "Here I stand." She is the immovable object to the Amazon's irresistible force. But don't mistake her stillness for passivity! She has plenty of fire in her, and when her rights are challenged, she will fight as fiercely as any warrior.

Shakuntala* is one of many Claimants, both female and male, portrayed in the great Indian epic the Mahabharata. Some hundred thousand verses long, dating in oral form to as early as 900 BCE, and comparable in richness and complexity to the *Iliad*, the Mahabharata takes its central theme from a question of succession. There is a king who falls in love with a fisher girl, whose father drives a hard bargain in the marriage negotiations: he insists that the throne pass to her future offspring and not to the king's existing son. The king agrees, thereby putting in motion a series of rifts that culminates in a massive war between two branches of the family several generations on. This main narrative, however, doesn't start until about two hundred pages in, and before that we get (among many other things) an account of the Bharata dynasty's founding, which also involves a question of succession. This is the story of Shakuntala.

When Shakuntala first arrives at the palace with her son, she is "recognized

---

* The name is pronounced Sha-KOON-tulla, with the *oo* as in *book*.

and admitted." In this ready welcome there may be a hint that her claim is known and credible to the public, or perhaps it's just that her ashram is respected; in any case, the gatekeepers let her in right away. She presents herself before the throne with poise. She asks the king to remember the promise he made six years ago and to consecrate the boy, who is described as shining with the brilliance of the morning sun, as his heir apparent. And according to the text, the king "remembered very well." Yet this is his response:

"I do not remember. Whose woman are you, evil ascetic? I do not recall ever having had any recourse to you ... Go or stay, as you please, or do what you want!"*

Shakuntala's first reaction reveals the Claimant's defining quality: **immovability**. Although stunned with shame, she stands still as a tree trunk. Her eyes grow red with fury, her lips tremble. She turns her head to look sidelong at the king (even three thousand years ago, side-eye was a thing) "with glances that seemed to burn him."[3] Early hearers of the story would have taken that last phrase as more than a metaphor; Shakuntala is an ascetic, and ascetics in India were understood to have accumulated spiritual heat, or *tapas*, from practicing austerities, just as bodybuilders accumulate physical strength from lifting weights. We can imagine the courtiers agog to see what will happen next: Will she run away? Fall to her knees wailing? Or—quite possibly, given her ascetic powers—blast the whole place to fiery smithereens?

Shakuntala does none of these things. In a moment she controls her expression, composes herself, and faces forward again, as is proper in the royal presence. Then she speaks:

You know very well, great king! Why do you say without concern that you do not know, lying like a commoner? Your heart knows the truth of it! Good sir, alas you yourself are the witness to your truth and your lie ... You think you are alone with yourself, but don't you

---

* How many times in human history has a woman with a child heard similar words of rejection? Two millennia later, denial of paternity would be the theme of Michael Jackson's No. 1 song "Billie Jean."

know the ancient seer who dwells in your heart? Him who knows your evil deeds? It is before him that you speak your lie![4]

Her words show another facet of the Claimant: her determination to stand **witness to the truth**, and to demand others do the same. In chapter 2 we saw how the Amazon charges ahead, certain of the justice of her cause. The Claimant takes that sense of certainty one step further: besides knowing when she is right, she knows when others are wrong—in particular, when they are lying—and she calls them on it, calls them to be witness to their own lies. "Your heart knows the truth of it," she says to King Dushanta. Imagine the confidence this must take, to presume to look into a king's heart and tell him, in front of his courtiers, exactly what's there. Like the Temptress and the Amazon, the Claimant knows what she wants and will not be turned from her course; more than her sisters, however, she believes in the plain power of the witness: the one who sees the truth, states the truth, and trusts that others, no matter their differing perspectives, will acknowledge the truth.

Shakuntala proceeds to deliver a lengthy discourse on the virtues of wives ("The wife is half the man, a wife is better than his best friend, a wife is the root of Law, Profit, and Love . . ."[5]) plus many arguments on behalf of her son. King Dushanta comes back with this:

> I do not know that this is my son you have born . . . women are liars—who will trust your word? Menaka, your mother, was a merciless slut who cast you off like a faded garland on a peak of the Himalayas. Vishvamitra, your merciless father, who, born a baron, reached for brahminhood, was a lecher. Menaka is the first of the Apsaras, Vishvamitra the first of the seers—how can you call yourself their daughter, speaking like a whore? Are you not ashamed to say such incredible things, especially in my presence? . . . Your own birth is very humble, and you look like a slut to me . . . I do not know you.[6]

Notice what the king is doing here. Aware of the story of Shakuntala's birth (her father was a famous sage, and her mother was a celestial, a spirit of the air, who was forced to give up her baby to a mortal family), he first reviles her parents as a fake brahmin and a slutty nymph who callously left her to be reared in an ashram. Who would trust the daughter of such scumbags? But in the next breath he lauds them as "the first of the Apsaras . . . the first of the seers" and marvels that she, a lowly ascetic, dares claim such high beings as her parents. He is trying to do what all gaslighters try to do: surround their target with a house of mirrors, twisting and contorting her situation until she doubts her sanity.

But it doesn't work on Shakuntala. Here's how she responds:

> King, you see the faults of others that are small, like mustard seeds, and you look but do not see your own, the size of pumpkins . . . My birth is higher than yours . . . You walk on earth, great king, but I fly the skies . . . Behold my power, great king!

> The lesson I shall teach you is the truth, impeccable prince, to instruct you, not to spite you, so listen and forbear. As long as an ugly man does not see his face in a mirror he will think that he is handsomer than others. But when he sees his ugly face in a mirror, he knows how inferior he is.[7]

Unfazed by the king's funhouse tricks, she turns the mirrors back on him. *Do you hear yourself? See yourself? Look here. See how ugly you have become. You are witness to your own lies.*

There's no gaslighting a Claimant.

Unlike the wild-at-heart Temptress and the iconoclastic Amazon, the Claimant is no rebel. She is a **conventionalist**, a champion of the established order, which holds covenants, particularly marriage covenants, in high esteem. Over millennia she has relied on society's respect for marriage and for the rights it confers on wives and mothers. Feminists today may counter that such rights come at the steep price of living under male control: "This so-called reverence for wives is just crumbs," they say, "thrown to us by men, who hold all the real power and would keep us docile by convincing us we're getting the best of the deal. Any woman who takes that deal is a dupe."

Is the Claimant just a patsy of the patriarchy? I don't think so. I think, rather, she is a woman with a keen sense of society's rules *and* the respect men have for those rules. So she follows the rules: she signs onto the team, shows up for practice without fail, plays her assigned position, and then, when it comes time to collect her reward, waves her contract in the team owner's face and dares him to break it. For thousands of years the main "position" women have been allowed to sign up for, hence their main basis for any claim of right, has been wife-mother; as we'll see in the next section, though, some of today's Claimants draw their power from other sources, other contracts. What all women of this type have in common is their unwavering insistence that, having played the game, they will not be denied their share of the prizes.

But back to our story. Having finished her speech, Shakuntala takes her son's hand and turns to walk away. At that moment, a "disembodied voice" sounds from above:

> Dushanta! Do not reject Shakuntala ... Shakuntala has spoken the truth. A wife bears a son by splitting her body in two; therefore, Dushanta, keep Shakuntala's son ... What man alive will forsake a live son born from himself?

The courtiers lift their eyes skyward, amazed. The king, however, seems relieved. *Yes*, he says with a smile. *The boy is my son. I knew it all along. I just needed everyone else to be convinced.* He "forgives" Shakuntala for her angry words (oh how she must have bitten her tongue at that!), accepting her as his wife and the boy as his heir. The people rejoice. And the great Bharata dynasty begins its roll through the ages, "radiant, divine, unvanquished."[8]

Some men are like King Dushanta: confronted by a woman with a righteous demand, they resist awhile but finally heed the voice of their conscience and bow to the truth it proclaims, perhaps with a face-saving "I knew it all along" and a magnanimous "I forgive you, dear." Other men, though they may bow, feel the loss of face so deeply they never forgive. In the next section, we'll meet one of those men.

Shauna: Unassailable

Shauna was a project manager at our company in the early 2000s. In her future were roles as a top-earning account executive and leader of sales teams, but back when she was a young job seeker, fresh out of university, she had little experience to go on. She had been an intern at one of our sister organizations and had set her sights on us. In her own words:

> I wanted to join this company. So I kept calling: "Good afternoon, Mike, how are you? You're back at the front desk again!" "Hello, Nigel, how was your weekend?" I saw it as like asking for a date: it was up to me to persuade them. I never felt entitled, so I didn't sound angry. My tone was "I would be really grateful if" versus "I am entitled to." I would ask, "Do you have any advice for how I could get through to [the head of HR]?" Finally they gave me to [a recruiter], who put me on the interview list for an entry-level role. The guys on the front desk were so nice to me. On my first day, I hugged them!

We can see hints of the Temptress in Shauna's relentless good cheer and daring deployment of relationship energy ("like asking for a date"). But Shauna's primary archetype was the Claimant: the woman who plants her feet and won't be budged—or ignored.

Shauna's nature became clear to me when, after a couple of years with the firm, she moved onto my R&D team. I had just been handed the task of planning the annual all-company meeting, a thankless assignment that required one to throw a Rolls-Royce event on a Honda Civic budget. Expecting to hear crickets, I sent out a call for helpers. Shauna volunteered right away. After looking over the initial spreadsheet I'd prepared, with line items for rooms, meals, transportation, and so on, she said: "I can do a lot better than this." She proceeded to make a series of deals with the hotel, airlines, shuttle companies, AV services, even down to the snack bags that would be handed to attendees when they checked in. No item was too small for her attention. She was a negotiating beast.

Past annual meetings had seen cost overruns of a hundred thousand, two hundred thousand, even half a million dollars. This one came in at fifty thousand dollars under budget.

Some years later, Shauna moved on to another organization. Now in a sales role, she had made an appointment with a prospective client, a bank executive. Upon arrival at his office, she—a 30ish Latina—was ushered into an imposing conference room where sat the client team: all men, all white, all over 50. The senior guy was on his phone, texting. Shauna greeted everyone, took her seat at the table, and waited.

"Thanks so much for coming, Shauna," said one of the men. "We can get started now."

"We can get started as soon as Jim is ready," Shauna said with a smile. "It's no problem. I'm happy to wait."

The underlings made a few more attempts to get going, which she politely brushed aside. She continued to sit, a pleasant expression on her face. The room grew quiet. Jim continued to tap on his phone. Finally noticing the strained silence, he looked up.

"Oh, we're fine to get started," he said. And the meeting began.

Telling me this story afterward, Shauna laughed. "They expected me just to start talking and be ignored," she said. "I wasn't going to have that. The only way to get his attention was to let things get extremely awkward. So, I waited him out."

Never get into a waiting contest with a Claimant. She'll always win.

Jim the bank executive was gracious in defeat, but when the stakes are higher than the minor matter of putting down a phone and paying attention, some men are anything but gracious. Case in point: Back when she was at the old company, Shauna had applied for her first sales job and been accepted. Amanda, our head of Global Sales, was eager to have her, and I, as her manager's manager, fully supported the move. What I wasn't aware of at the time was the salary negotiation Shauna had initiated. It turns out she had an offer in hand from another consulting firm, one for a lot more money than she'd been making and more than Amanda was prepared to give. When Shauna asked Amanda to help her understand why she should take less, Amanda conceded the point and went on to talk about the relationships Shauna had built at the firm and the product knowledge she had already acquired, hence the bigger commissions she could make right off the bat. Shauna wasn't convinced. After thinking it over, Amanda said she'd be willing to go up a bit, but that Shauna would need to get approval from Bruce, the company president.

As Shauna tells it: "I went into the meeting with Bruce very prepared. I was direct about my request. I did feel entitled, but I felt I had a right to be. I had that offer in hand; I'd been validated by the market. And Amanda had made it clear how much she wanted me."

Bruce was not happy. He told Shauna he didn't think she should be paid that much. But Shauna knew she was on solid ground: Amanda wanted her, she had that other offer, she was willing to walk away, and she saw no reason to cave. She stood firm. After some discussion, Bruce approved the higher salary.

Several months after that, the sales force gathered for a meeting. During evening festivities at the hotel bar, Shauna found herself at a table with Bruce. He'd had a few drinks. The conversation turned to her previous pay negotiations.

"I can't believe how you treated me," he said.

"What do you mean?" she said.

"You knew what you wanted, and you weren't going to budge." He leaned forward, his finger jabbing. "You know what you did? You put me over a barrel and ass-fucked me."

Shauna didn't quite know how to respond.

Here's what she said to me about the incident, years later:

> When Bruce said, "You knew what you wanted, and weren't going to budge," my thought was: "That's a good negotiator!" But he felt insulted. Here was a woman asking for power. How dare I? I wasn't

one of his drinking buddies, slapping him on the back and going to ball games. I had to make a business case, and I made it well. He said my preparation made me "unassailable." I had never realized that being unassailable is insulting to someone who is *not* prepared. They consider it an unfair advantage.

Shauna's story rang true to me. Bruce was notoriously unprepared, and (I recalled with some amusement) he had made an identical comment to me after a budget meeting at around that same time: "Jocelyn," he'd said in an exasperated tone, "the way you lay everything out in such detail, it's *unassailable.*" His irritation was clear, but so was his grudging respect—respect that was apparent, too, in his crude remark to Shauna.

Men like Bruce have a hard time with the Claimant: she threatens them by holding them to account and giving them no toehold, no reason to dismiss her requests or throw her out. That's why, when we're confronted with a man like Bruce who sees life as a dominance game, the Claimant may be our best role model. There is some risk, of course. If we waver, if we show the smallest crack, such a man will seize upon it. But if we can remain solid as a rock and clear as a mirror, utterly prepared and utterly confident in the justice of our claim, then, like Shauna, we may be truly unassailable.

Learning from the Claimant

How can you emulate the Claimant without risking too much? Here are two ways.

Strengthen your BATNA. In their 1981 classic *Getting to Yes*, Roger Fisher and William L. Ury introduced the concept of a BATNA: best alternative to a negotiated agreement. Your BATNA is what you must do or accept should you and your adversary fail to come to terms. If your BATNA is weak (that is, undesirable) you have less leverage in the negotiation; if it is strong, more leverage. Therefore, you want your BATNA to be as strong as it can be.

Think about buying a used car. Scenario 1: Your old car has died, your city has terrible public transportation, your boss won't give you any time off, and you don't know anyone who has a car you can borrow long-term. If you don't reach an agreement with this seller, your only option is to scour the listings and run around town in hopes of finding something cheaper, *today*. In this scenario, your BATNA is weak and your power limited. (This, by the way, was the very situation in which I found myself thirty years ago in Los Angeles, when I ended up paying $2,700 for a 1969 Volkswagen Beetle with recurring engine problems, the repairs for which, over the time I owned it, must have cost that much again. Good thing the Bug had charm!)

Scenario 2: Your existing car is getting a bit shabby, and you'd like a newer one. There's no rush: the old one works fine, and should it conk out unexpectedly, your wife has one she doesn't use much and is happy to lend you for the occasional errands that, given you work from home, are all you really need wheels for. You aren't fussy about makes and models. You visit a nearby dealer and one car strikes your fancy, but the price seems high. "I'll come back another time," you say to the salesman as you and your wife walk away, debating where to go for lunch. "Wait!" says the guy, running after you. "Let me see what I can do."

Walk away—that's the option a woman with a strong BATNA has. It gives her tremendous power. When King Dushanta calls Shakuntala a lying slut, she knows she can take her son and return to the ashram where she'll be welcome to stay for life; so, having made her speech, she turns to leave, and it's at that moment the "disembodied voice" pipes up to tell the king to do the right thing. Shauna, in her negotiations with Bruce, knew she had another offer in hand—an offer for more money, from a company she'd have been happy to join—giving her the means to exit in complete security. We who would be Claimants like Shakuntala and Shauna must ensure that walking away is a great option for us, too. If it isn't, and if we can find no way to make it so, we had better make a new plan.

Play by the rules. The Amazon, if she's to be successful, must have allies; Lysistrata, you'll recall, spent time lining up her fellow sex-strikers before pursuing her anti-war cause. The Claimant does without allies. She is not a cause-fighter but a rights-demander, and though there may be times when she demands rights for others—her children, for instance—those rights are always an extension of her own. Like the Snow Queen, her opposite on the archetypes wheel, the Claimant is a solo act.

In place of allies, the Claimant has The Rules: the established order with its norms, customs, and laws. Set up by men and revered by men, The Rules are the sword and shield of the woman who stands alone seeking justice from the patriarchy. Woe to any Claimant who *hasn't* followed The Rules, for she'll face rejection or worse. Imagine if Shakuntala had been unfaithful to the king, had created even a whiff of impropriety, before showing up at court with her son. Imagine if she hadn't insisted on his marrying her in the first place! And what if Shauna hadn't followed the correct process for applying for a new internal role but instead had gone straight to Bruce, waving her job offer and listing her demands? Suffice to say, things wouldn't have worked out.

The would-be Claimant must be able to point to her unblemished record, the commitments she has kept, and the authorities who will back her up. She must be able to say—as Catherine of Aragon, a consummate Claimant, said to Henry VIII when he tried to annul their marriage—"For every scholar that would vote for you, I could find a thousand that would vote for me."

We women sometimes look askance at our successful sisters who play by the rules. "Climbers," we call them. "Brownnosers." We prefer the rebels. But nine times out of ten a rebellious woman, unless she has allies, is a woman about to be sacked. Over the years, I've grown more admiring of the non-rebel: the woman who stands strong and still, still as a tree trunk, secure in the knowledge that her contract is unbroken and her claim is righteous.

PART TWO

EARTH-WATER

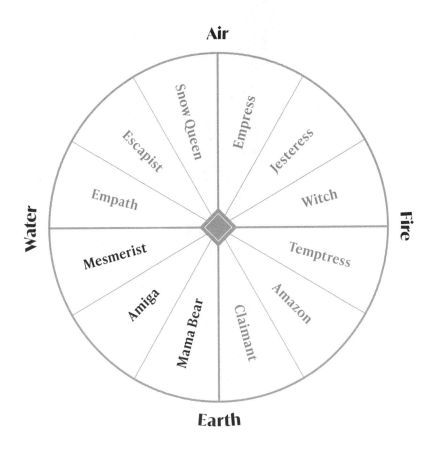

4

THE MAMA BEAR

REBEKAH AND JACOB TIPTOE TO the tent flap and lean close to hear what's happening inside. Jacob's brother Esau is in there; he entered a few moments ago, carrying a bowl of savory stew, prepared from a brace of hare shot that morning, to give to his father.

The eavesdroppers have missed Esau's words of greeting, but now they hear old Isaac say, "Who are you?" Isaac is blind and, increasingly these days, confused.

"Father, I am Esau, your eldest son," says Esau. "Remember, you asked me to shoot game and prepare you a meal, that you might bless me before you die. Remember, Father?"

There is a short silence. Then Isaac, his voice quavering, says: "Yes, but—who was that, the one who was here before? He brought food. I ate it. I blessed him. Who was that?"

Outside the tent, Jacob flinches. Rebekah grips his shoulder.

"Father?" Esau's voice is suddenly high, anxious. "Father, what are you saying?"

"He brought food. I gave him the eldest son's blessing. I made him lord over his brothers. I gave him the … all the … who *was* that? Was it not you, Esau?"

"Not me." Esau's voice sinks to a low growl. "Jacob. It was Jacob."

"Eh? Jacob? Well … I blessed *him*. He has the blessing. I can't do anything about it now." Loud sniffs. "What's that, stew? I could eat again. Give it here, boy. Here. Ah, that's good."

A great and bitter cry shakes the air: "No! Bless me, even me also, O my father!"

In response there's a sound of slurping. Outside the tent, Jacob turns worried eyes to his mother. With a smile and a nod, Rebekah leads her favorite son away.

Rebekah: Mother of Ten Thousands

Manipulator. That's the epithet that gets thrown at our three earth-water archetypes, including the one who is the focus of this chapter. And perhaps she deserves the name, for no warm fuzzy, Grandma Bear is she, dispensing hugs all round, but a strong and wily Mama Bear, willing to risk all for her cubs yet unwilling to let those cubs bumble or fritter their lives away. If there are rumps to be kicked, she'll kick them. If there are schemes to arrange, she'll arrange them. And she has no qualms about judging one cub superior to the rest.

Rebekah, the wife of Isaac in the Hebrew Bible, is a quintessential Mama Bear. She plays a prominent role in Genesis—so prominent that the famous "God of Abraham, Isaac, and Jacob" might more accurately be called the God of Abraham, *Rebekah*, and Jacob. Her story unfolds in three episodes: a marriage, a pregnancy, and a trick.

In Genesis 24 we learn that Sarah, the wife of Abraham, has recently died and that their son, Isaac, is 40 years of age and still unmarried. The family is living in Canaan, a few weeks' journey from their ancestral home; Abraham, not wanting a foreigner for a daughter-in-law, decides to send a servant back to the old country to find a wife for Isaac. The servant makes the trip. Arriving at a well near a prosperous settlement, he encounters Rebekah and begs leave to water his camels. Though the man is a stranger, Rebekah insists on watering his beasts herself. *Such hospitality*, he thinks; *this woman is the one.* He proceeds to put the marriage proposal to her mother and brother, who agree, stipulating only a delay of ten days to prepare. But the servant doesn't want to delay, so they call Rebekah and ask her wishes. *Yes*, she says, not hesitating; *I will go.* As she departs with her nurse and maids, the whole group riding on camels, her brother and mother bless her, saying: "Our sister, be the mother of thousands of ten thousands; and may your descendants possess the gate of those who hate them!" (24:60)[1]

Arriving back in Canaan, the party is met by Abraham and Isaac. Isaac takes Rebekah into his tent; she becomes his wife, and (the text says) he loves her. The episode concludes with this odd remark: "So Isaac was comforted after his mother's death." (24:67) Is he "comforted" because Rebekah will take his mother's place, ruling him as Sarah once ruled him?

The second episode occurs in Genesis 25. Isaac and Rebekah have now been married for twenty years, during which time they have had no children, but Isaac prays to God, and Rebekah finally conceives twins. The babies struggle together in her womb, making her pregnancy an ordeal. "If it is thus, why do I live?" she cries, and she sets off "to inquire of the Lord." (25:22) Notice her bold directness: unlike her husband, who *prays* to God, she *makes inquiry* of God, as one might of a government official. (I imagine her standing before a stone altar under the sky, proudly erect, just as Shakuntala stood before the king's throne.) And God answers her as directly: "Two nations are in your womb, and two peoples, born of you, shall be divided; the one shall be stronger than the other, the elder shall serve the younger." (25:23)

When Rebekah gives birth, the first child comes out red and hirsute. She names him Esau, which means *hairy* or *rough*. The second child comes out clutching Esau's heel; she names him Jacob, which means *he supplants*. When the boys grow up, Esau becomes a skillful hunter, a man of the field, but Jacob is "a quiet man, dwelling in tents." (25:27) Isaac loves Esau, because Esau provides him with delicious things to eat, but Rebekah prefers Jacob—a preference that, given what we already know of her character, seems unlikely to be capricious.

Next there's a short incident in which Rebekah does not appear, yet her presence is felt. One evening, we are told, Jacob has baked some bread and prepared a lentil pottage for his supper. His brother Esau returns from hunting. We get this exchange:

Esau: Let me eat some of that red pottage, for I am famished!

Jacob: First, sell me your birthright.

Esau: I am about to die; of what use is a birthright to me?

Jacob: Swear to me first. (25:30)

Esau swears it, and Jacob hands over the food. "Thus," the text says, "Esau despised his birthright." From this anecdote we get the distinct sense that Esau is a slave to his appetites and none too bright. We are also led to wonder what—or rather, who—put it in Jacob's head to demand his brother's birthright in payment for a bowl of pottage.

The final episode in Rebekah's story is the tricking of Isaac. Very old now, Isaac tells Esau to go hunt game and prepare his favorite food: "Bring it to me that I may eat," he says, "that I may bless you before I die." (27:4) Esau dutifully takes his quiver and bow and departs for the fields. But Rebekah has been listening; she seeks out Jacob, and this conversation ensues:

Rebekah: Now, my son, obey my word as I command you. Go to the flock, and fetch me two good kids, that I may prepare from them savory food for your father, such as he loves; and you shall bring it to your father to eat, so that he may bless you before he dies.

Jacob: Behold, my brother is a hairy man, and I am a smooth man. Perhaps my father will feel me, and I shall seem to be mocking him, and bring a curse upon myself and not a blessing.

Rebekah: Upon me be your curse, my son; only obey my word, and go, fetch them to me. (27:9-13)

Once the kids are killed, Rebekah skins them. Then she dresses Jacob in Esau's best tunic, wrapping the goatskins on his arms and neck so as to mimic his brother's hairiness. She gives Jacob the stew she has prepared and tells him to take it to his father.

The ruse goes off perfectly. Blind old Isaac isn't sure at first, but when Jacob kneels before him and he feels the hairy skins, he's convinced, and upon the one whom he believes to be his eldest son he bestows the traditional blessing that makes the recipient his successor, patriarch of the family and inheritor of all wealth. Some hours later Esau returns from hunting, prepares his own stew, and takes it to Isaac in good faith. We've seen what happens next.

But Rebekah isn't done yet. She tells Jacob that his brother is angry now (with good reason!) and may mean to kill him. He needs to go–to his uncle, back in the old country. "Stay with [Laban] a while," she says, "until your brother's fury turns away and he forgets what you have done to him; then I will send, and fetch you from there." (27: 44-45) But only Isaac has the authority to send Jacob away, so Rebekah invents a reason for Isaac's ears: *Jacob shouldn't marry a Canaanite woman; he must go home and get himself a proper wife.*

Isaac, as usual, falls for it. Summoning Jacob, he says: *I've decided you shall not marry a Canaanite woman. You must go to your uncle's house. Find a wife there.*

So Jacob goes, and Esau the Disinherited is left behind to nurse his hurts, his cry of "Bless me, even me also, O my father!" set to echo down the ages as one of the great cries of betrayal: a brother betrayed by his brother, yes, but also a son betrayed by his mother, who planned the whole thing.

In light of Rebekah's story, let's consider three key attributes of the Mama Bear.

First, she **leads via her children**. From the day Rebekah's mother and brother send her off with the blessing, "Our sister, be the mother of thousands of ten thousands; and may your descendants possess the gate of those who hate them!" we know she is destined to be not only a mother of many but also a mother of power: powerful leaders, that is, whose glory will redound to her. Her progeny's achievements will be her achievements, their fame her fame. Today we might see this as a sign of oppression: "If all her status comes from her children (and that really means her sons), then she has no status of her own." But this is to misunderstand the nature of power and leadership. As I discuss in two of my previous books,* true power is the ability to *get work done*, and true leadership means getting work done *through others*. The strong leader is not the one who dominates a weak and dependent tribe, but the one who creates a strong tribe capable of acting independently. Until quite recently, a woman's tribe could only be that created from her womb: her children, their children, their spouses, and so on. If this tribe, of which she was the matriarch, grew powerful, she could rightly claim its power for her own—especially if, like Rebekah, she had shaped its leadership from the start.

Which brings us to the Mama Bear's second attribute: she **plays favorites**. Most people think the first rule of parenthood is to love all one's children the same, that to play favorites is to be a bad mother. And indeed, the preference Rebekah shows her younger son, to the point of scheming to deny her older son his birthright, may raise eyebrows. But does it mean her love is bestowed unequally on the two? I don't think so. If we consider her as the founder of a great organization (the nation of Israel), her actions appear in a different light.

Remember that Esau and Jacob are twins, born in the same hour, Esau only technically the elder. Also remember that Esau is a bit of dimwit, while Jacob (as the rest of his story in the Bible makes plain) is anything but. Finally remember that their father Isaac, who at the age of 40 was not even trusted by his own father to go pick out his own wife, is consistently shown to be a man of limp will and dubious judgment, led by his appetites as Esau is. All this to say, Rebekah not only knows which of her sons is best suited to

---

* *The Greats on Leadership* and *The Art of Quiet Influence* (Nicholas Brealey Publishing, 2016 and 2019)

occupy the patriarch's seat, she also knows who must take the initiative to put him there. In arranging for Jacob to succeed his father, she is doing what any good founder does: choosing the right person to lead the organization into the future. And we know God agrees with her choice, for God told her so.

The third attribute of a Mama Bear is the **absolute responsibility** she takes for outcomes. When Jacob worries he'll bring a curse upon himself should his father discover his deceit, Rebekah reassures him with, "Upon me be your curse, my son." Her words remind me of my mother telling me as a teenager that I could always use her as an excuse for getting out of things. "Just tell them your mother won't let you," she'd say. "I don't mind being the bad guy."

The Mama Bear never minds being the bad guy. In this respect she is unlike the Temptress and the Amazon, who tend not to worry about the negative fallout of their actions; once they've decided on a path they charge ahead, confident it will all work out. The Mama Bear does not lack confidence, but she has a keener sense than her archetypal sisters that it may *not* all work out and that someone, in the not-unlikely case of disaster, will need to shoulder the blame. With "let the curse fall on me," Rebekah provides cover for Jacob—the same sort of cover a good leader of the present day provides for her subordinates. Let's meet such a leader now.

Renee: A Mom with Drive

It was sometime in the early 1980s when John, our company founder and CEO, interviewed Renee for a sales manager position. Renee was a stay-at-home mom who had never held a professional job, and John was hesitant. She persuaded him to give her a try on a commission-only basis: she'd get no salary, only a cut of the revenue her sales team brought in. If they didn't perform, she'd be paid nothing. I've wondered if that unusual start gave rise to her often-demonstrated belief that her success and her people's success were the same.

About Renee the Mama Bear I want to relate just one story, about a competitive sales pitch she orchestrated in 1996. At the time she was head of our company's largest division: the "big horse," as John the CEO called it. On the pitch team were a couple of my friends, Liz and Daniel. It's they who later told me about it.

The day before the pitch, our team gathered in the New York office to prepare. The client, a global professional services firm I'll call DLT, wanted a comprehensive training curriculum for new associates all the way up to partners, a piece of business worth a million dollars with potential for more. Our company hadn't ever put together an offering of such magnitude; we had a set of standard training programs we could customize, and we had some consulting capabilities, but that's about it. This would be new territory for us.

The prep meeting got underway with our team of eight or nine seated around the conference table. Renee was up and moving, energy high, eyes wide: picture a 50-year-old Nancy Pelosi with short, fluffy, ash-blonde hair. There was talk about the solution we were to propose; there was talk about the agenda the client had prescribed and the slide deck we had created. Then someone asked this question: *How do we want DLT to see us?*

Renee stopped, fixed the room with her big eyes, and said, "We want to be their general contractor."

There were confused looks. No one had heard that term applied to our work before. But Renee laid it out, and by the end of the meeting everyone was aligned behind this new vision. Here's how Liz, quite junior at the time, described the experience:

> Renee had all our attention and respect. It was the most choreographed pitch I had ever been part of.

> She said, "Here's how the client is going to *know* we can be their general contractor." Each person's role was planned: what you'd say, how you'd say it. Renee didn't leave a single stone unturned. But she didn't do the high-pressure "we have to wow them" thing; she never created a sense of panic. It was more like, "We can, and

we will." She was completely clear and confident, and she instilled that sense in us.

It was a level of direction I'd never gotten from anyone else. And I would have followed her off the end of a dock.

"As the planning meeting was wrapping up," Liz recalled, "I suddenly realized I had no idea how to introduce myself. I was that green. I decided it would be worse to look a fool in front of the client than to look a fool now, so I spoke up: I asked Renee what I should say."

Renee took the time right then to help Liz plan out exactly how she would introduce herself. "She didn't brush me off as too junior to matter," said Liz. "She gave me a sense of importance. Basically, she taught me to walk and talk."

There was an expression at our company: "the School of Renee." Certain people were in that school or were alums of it. Others were not, for like all Mama Bears, Renee played favorites. She liked smart people and people who were good with clients; her main criterion for accepting you as her student, however, was whether you were *willing*. She had no time for those who said, "I can't" or "I won't," but as long as you said, "I can" or "I'll try," she would welcome you with warm affection, burnished by clear direction and sound advice. And we, the pupils in her school, were like the little mallards in *Make Way for Ducklings*, marching proudly along behind her, ready to follow her off the dock.

Daniel, another member of the DLT pitch team, put it this way: "Renee never threatened or harangued. She told you what was expected and conveyed her absolute confidence in you. She always made you feel like, 'She's got it; she has my back; now I just have to live up to it.'"

Back to that sales pitch: The next morning, the team piled into a couple of taxis and set off for the client's office. In the cab with Renee were Liz and Daniel, hunkered in the back seat, white-knuckled as they tore through New York traffic. Renee was perched in the front seat, getting her game face on, not breaking a sweat.

They arrived at the site. The client had decreed each vendor team should have exactly one hour: when the 60 minutes were up, a bell would go off, and no matter where they were in their presentation, the vendors would need to exit through the door on the left as the next team entered through the door on the right. Under Renee's guidance, our crew had rehearsed rigorously—not for a scripted performance, but for an improvisation, with each person knowing what he or she was accountable for—and they were confident they had the timing down. As the meeting proceeded, everything seemed to be going according to plan.

Also in the room was John, our founder-CEO. Renee had prepped him for his role: as owner of the top-to-top client relationship he would be ready to talk about how we'd work with DLT strategically, over the long term. With five or six minutes to go until the bell, the senior-most client asked that very question: "Tell us how you'll work with us over time. Have you had this type of strategic relationship with other organizations?"

John, hearing his cue, got up and stepped to the front. "Let me share a few examples," he said. An expert and eager storyteller, John could go on at length once he got started, and as the time to conclude drew near, it was obvious he was just getting warmed up. Here's how Daniel described the scene:

> There was a clock on the wall behind John. Everyone could see it ticking down: four minutes . . . three minutes . . . two minutes. Amanda [the account executive] was staring frantically at Renee and tapping her wrist. Nobody knew what to do. John showed no signs of stopping.

> With half a minute to go, Renee stood, walked to the front of the room, put her hand on John's shoulder, and said with a big smile: ". . . and we will be *so happy* to share more of these stories with you, should we have the honor of working with you."

At that precise moment, the bell went off. We rose, thanked them, and exited stage left.

We won the business. Afterward, one of the clients confided that that final moment was one of the reasons they went with us. "When Renee got up and stopped your founder in mid-sentence," she said, "it told us everything we needed to know about how you would respect us; how you would put our agenda first."

A Mama Bear will never hesitate to stop the founder in mid-sentence, because to her, the founder is just another one of her kids, as much in need of direction and coaching as any kid. Of course she wants to support the team; more than that, however, she wants the team to *win*, and she'll do whatever cuffing, cajoling, or restraining is necessary to that end.

"Renee was a truly caring person," said Liz, "but I would never paint her as warm and fuzzy. She wasn't the mom with a shoulder to cry on. She was the mom with drive."

Learning from the Mama Bear

Rebekah had sons; Renee had employees. You don't need actual children to be a Mama Bear, only a Mama Bear's attitude toward those around you. Here are three ways to demonstrate that fierce yet nurturing outlook.

Identify with your team's success. Just about anyone in a leadership role will pay lip service to the principle "My job is to help my people succeed." Few leaders, however, act like they really believe it—not consistently, anyway. We all harbor a secret or not-so-secret hope that being a leader means we can call the shots: see *our* ideas appreciated, *our* plans carried out, *our* talents applauded.

But that hope is mostly vain. As I explain in *The Art of Quiet Influence*, leaders can only succeed through their people; moreover, to quote the great Taoist sage Laozi, "of the best leader, when his work is done, the people all say, 'We did it ourselves.'" It is one of the paradoxes of leadership that the more you seek to dominate others, the smaller they become, hence the smaller *you* become. Conversely, the more you build up others to be big without you, the bigger a leader you are. Renee had a visceral sense of all this; it's why she never instilled fear in her "kids," only confidence, using a formula of equal parts clear direction and relentless encouragement. And when one of her kids hit a home run, her delight was real.

Treat them differently. In his business classic *First, Break All the Rules*, Marcus Buckingham theorizes that excellent managers don't treat everyone the same; instead, they revel in individuality, giving to and demanding from each employee what is fitting and capitalizing on each employee's strengths. The Mama Bear (who, incidentally, may be the best *manager* of our twelve archetypes) would agree. Rebekah, aware of her sons' differing talents and dispositions, treats them differently—some would say unfairly, but then, would it not have been more unfair for Jacob, clearly the superior leader, to be denied his birthright as such? And if Esau had received everything he was supposedly owed, how happy would he really have been? Note that when Jacob finally returns from his uncle's house to take up his patriarchal position, Esau runs to meet him, falls on his neck and kisses him. Jacob and his family all bow to Esau and offer him a rich gift (of land? livestock? we're not told), but Esau says, "I have enough, my brother; keep what you have for yourself." (33:9) Esau, it seems, is content and thriving in the place his mother so "unfairly" created for him.

Schooled as most of us are in the Western management precept that the same rules apply to everyone, we may be reluctant to adopt a Mama Bear's outlook. Where we can start without fear of being accused of undue partiality is by studying our team members' talents, skills, personalities, and preferences so we can place them in roles that allow them to shine and, maybe more important, keep them out of roles they're no good at. Even if we're not a formal boss, we can still take a talent-developer's attitude; for example, by praising a colleague's unique skill that has gone unnoticed, or by requesting a colleague for a project we're managing. Renee was never my boss, but she used to tout me and my abilities to the powers on high, and whenever our paths crossed she would give me a dose of her wide-eyed, confidence-boosting energy. To a Mama Bear, anyone can be a cub.

Take the blame. When Jacob worries his deceit will draw down his father's wrath, possibly even God's wrath, Rebekah doesn't hesitate. *Upon me be the curse*, she says. *Go get the goats, Jacob; we're doing this.* Rebekah's active, decisive nature was evident from the start of her story: recall that when her mother and brother wanted to delay her departure for her marriage and Abraham's emissary objected, the choice was put to her, and she said at once, *I will go.* But many of the archetypes are active and decisive. What sets the Mama Bear apart is her willingness—nay, her insistence—that she'll take any blame coming down.

This seemingly masochistic strategy is actually empowering, for the person who says *upon me be the curse* becomes a person with followers. The would-be leader who thinks it's enough to announce a direction in a firm tone fails to understand what Renee and Rebekah understand: people rarely have the courage to march out on a new path as long as they fear they might suddenly look around and find that, like Wile E. Coyote, they're standing alone in midair about to take a massive fall. But when a leader assuages their fear, saying, "Don't worry, I'll cover you," then, wow—watch how fast they'll take that new path, confident that their mama's got their back.

5

THE AMIGA

Yama [the god of death]: Return, go, Savitri! Perform his funeral rites. You are acquitted of all debt to your husband; you have gone as far as you can.

Savitri: Where my husband goes, there I too must go; this is the ancient and eternal Law. By my austerities, by my conduct toward my teachers, by my vow proceeding from love of my husband, and just as much by your grace, unobstructed is my course. The wise, seeing the truth, have declared a fellow walker to be a friend. Having invoked your friendship, anything I say, that you must hear.

Not lacking in self-control, but practicing the Law and austerities in the forest... the virtuous say the Law comes first.

Yama: I am pleased with your speech, which unites sound, word, meaning, and reason. Choose a boon now, excepting your

husband's life; let me grant you any boon, irreproachable woman.
(Mahabharata, 3(42)281.20–25)[1]

Savitri: Friend of the Devil

In Indian popular culture, Princess Savitri—who, legend says, followed after the god of death and pleaded with him, successfully, to spare her husband's life—is a symbol of wifely devotion. During the Hindu festival named for her, married women pray for their husbands to enjoy long life. The cover of one contemporary book adaptation, *The Triumph of Love*, shows a doe-eyed Savitri leaning down to kiss her dead husband's lips; she's also the heroine of several Bollywood romances. But her story as first told in the Mahabharata* is only incidentally about romantic love. In essence, it is about an alliance masterfully made.

In the original tale, Savitri is an unmarried princess bidden by her father to go forth and find a husband. She returns after months of searching and announces her choice: Prince Satyavat, the impoverished son of a blind, dethroned king. Satyavat's foretold future is even less promising: exactly one year hence he will die, the manner unspecified. Savitri marries him anyway. She leaves her home and joins Satyavat and his parents in the "forest of austerities," where they all live as hermits, praying and studying. She comports herself flawlessly. As the one-year mark approaches, having told no one what she knows of her husband's coming demise, she undertakes a vow whereby she stands upright, alone and fasting, for three days and nights.†

At last the dreaded hour arrives. Savitri accompanies Satyavat to chop wood in the forest, and when (as she has expected) he collapses, she rests

---

* The Mahabharata is the same epic that contains the story of Shakuntala; see chapter 3.
† Ancient Hindu culture regarded such austerities as spiritual and moral strength-building exercises. The discipline required to perform them was seen as a mark of existing virtue and a developer of greater virtue.

his head in her lap and waits. Yama, the god of death, appears, "yellow-robed and turbaned, radiant like the sun, brilliantly black . . . terrifying." (281.8–9) He draws out Satyavat's soul, fetters it with a noose, and sets out along the road to the underworld. Savitri, "the vow-perfected woman," follows step for step.

And now begins a series of exchanges between the god and the princess, each of which follows the same pattern: he tells her to turn back, she refuses and proceeds to deliver a short speech seemingly unrelated to the situation at hand, whereupon he expresses pleasure in her words and tells her to ask a boon—anything, he says, except her husband's life. What may surprise us, if we have heard modern versions of the story, is that there isn't a hint of "pleading" on Savitri's part; rather, each of her speeches consists of a flat statement that she will stay with her husband as prescribed by the ancient and eternal Law, followed by her thoughts on an elite group of people she calls "the virtuous" and the friendship that exists among them.* Moreover, she invokes *Yama's* friendship as a reason for him to listen to her: "The wise, seeing the truth, have declared a fellow walker to be a friend," she says. "Having invoked your friendship, anything I say, that you must hear." (281.22)

How extraordinary, this claim of friendship with the god of death! In it we see the foremost quality of the Amiga archetype: she is **alliance-minded**. In any situation, no matter how fraught with conflict or hostility, the Amiga will default to seeking out shared interests and areas of alignment, then set about emphasizing those meeting points. For the Amiga, there are no real enemies: only adversaries, who in her view are allies-in-waiting, ripe for conversion. The Devil himself is no exception.

Let's see how Savitri forges this unlikely alliance as she continues, step by step, along the forest path. "Choose a boon," Yama has said, so she asks for her father-in-law to regain his sight. Yama agrees. Again he tells her to turn back; again, she refuses, saying her course is fixed: she must follow her

---

* The Sanskrit word I translate as "the virtuous" is *satya* or *sattva*. Other possible translations are "the strict," "the just," "the true," "the worthy," "the wise," or "the excellent."

husband as *dharma*, or Law, requires.* She delivers another short speech about the virtuous, this time praising their loyalty to spouses and the benefits of their companionship. Yama is impressed anew. "Pleasant and mind-expanding are the precepts you state, a trove of good advice," he says, and offers to grant her a second boon—anything but Satyavat's life. She asks for her father-in-law's kingdom to be restored to him. Yama grants the favor.

With the third cycle, Savitri begins to preface each of her discourses with a bit of praise for Yama, implying that he, too, is a member of that admirable set known as the virtuous. "These creatures are restrained by you according to rule," she says, "and having restrained them, you lead them, and not by whim. Therefore your greatness is celebrated." It's a wonderfully subtle way of aligning herself with the lord of death, who, we may imagine, must grow pretty sick of us humans weeping and wailing at his terrible capriciousness, when from his perspective he's only doing his job in executing (pun intended) the laws of nature. Savitri is flattering him, but it's not only that; she's also placing the two of them in the same club, the League of the Virtuous. *You and I*, she suggests, *aren't like* some *people, idling about and succumbing to the whim of the moment. You and I are masters of our souls: impartial, disciplined, austere.* "With restraint and Law are your people imbued," she says. It goes without saying that she is one of his people.

Yama is delighted to find such a friend. "Like as water to a thirsty man, so are these words you utter," he says. This woman gets him! How different she is from other mortals, who fear his approach, doing anything to escape him. Savitri isn't the least afraid; she actually seems to enjoy his company. And she isn't begging for her husband's life (so irritating when wives do that—as if he, a god, would be swayed by human tears). She's just conversing, and with such good sense. "From friendship for all creatures a trustworthy reputation is born," she says; "therefore in the virtuous, especially, the world places trust." (281.40) Never has Yama heard the like.

The **giving of trust** is one of the chief ways the Amiga expresses her

---

* *Dharma*, usually translated as "the Law," can also mean "justice," "righteousness," "goodness," "virtue," or "the Way."

alliance-mindedness. Notice that Savitri is not asking Yama to trust *her* so much as implying that she trusts *him*; trusts him because he is one of the virtuous, who may always be counted on to do the right thing. It's the same technique used by con artists. The confidence man does not, as most people think, ask you to place your confidence in him, but the reverse: he places his confidence in *you*—by, for example, asking you to hold a large sum of money in your bank account until he can retrieve it. "I trust you," he says. "I know you won't rip me off." Manipulative? Sure, and when a con man does it, usually criminal. But the Amiga's intent, though arguably self-serving, is not to deceive or take advantage. Rather, she seeks to convert adversaries to allies by *being* an ally: getting on the same side, seeing things their way, and highlighting how two sets of interests align.

In Savitri's approach we also see a third quality of the Amiga: her **appreciation** for others, even when there seems little to appreciate. Most of us would be hard-pressed to find anything nice to say about a demon dragging our spouse down to the underworld, but Savitri does: *You walk the straight and narrow, Yama,* she says. *You stick to the rules. I admire that.* Appreciation is incredibly disarming, especially when the other person is used to the opposite. I recall the words of wisdom I once received from a college professor to whom I was complaining about an obnoxious (I thought) fellow student who seemed impervious to attempts to shut him down. "Fighting with him isn't going to work," said my professor, "because for him, a fight is just a normal interaction. He's used to it, so he'll keep punching back." When I shifted to a more appreciative mode, the obnoxious student almost immediately changed his tone, becoming—toward me, anyway—far more open and conciliatory. Apparently, the Amiga's techniques work on both mortals and immortals.

Yama continues to lead Satyavat's soul away. Savitri continues to follow them and discourse on virtue, thereby earning more boons. For the third boon, she asks for her father to have a hundred sons; for the fourth, that she herself give birth to a hundred sons—by Satyavat. We can see how the favors she asks, though still conforming to Yama's exception, are driving ever nearer to her goal: to win back Satyavat's life. Yama keeps telling her to turn around, and on the fifth cycle she doesn't even bother to say no, instead launching right into this speech:

> The virtuous are always in an eternal state of law; the virtuous neither despair nor tremble. The meeting of the virtuous with the virtuous is never fruitless; from the virtuous, the virtuous find no danger.

> Knowing this is the conduct practiced eternally by the noble, the virtuous act for the sake of another without looking for recompense. And no favor among the virtuous is fruitless; moreover, no purpose will be unsuccessful. Because this steadiness is eternal among the virtuous, they are the guardians. (281.46–49)

Overcome with admiration, Yama replies: "Since you speak united with the Law, pleasing to the mind, well-grounded, full of meaning, therefore my faith in you is supreme. Choose an incomparable boon, O Diligent Devotion!"

He fails to add, "excepting Satyavat's life."

Savitri pounces. "You make no exception to your favor—not a single one, as in the other boons, my sweet!" she says, triumph resounding through her words. "So the boon I choose is this: *This Satyavat shall live!*"

Yama is caught. He must grant her request. Indeed, we might suspect him of *wanting* to grant it—not only because he is virtuous but because this supremely virtuous woman sees and appreciates his virtue. "So be it," he says; and the King of the Law, loosening the noose, releases his prisoner to his new ally. The narrator says he does it "with a joyful heart." *

Contrary to how the story is often told today, Savitri has engaged in not one moment of pleading. What propelled her along the road of death was her devotion to her husband. What won him back from the god of death was the alliance she forged so brilliantly.

---

* "O Diligent Devotion!" could also be translated as "O object of my devotion!"—which would provide further textual evidence that Yama wants to grant Savitri's wish and therefore omits his standard exception.

Sabrina: Walking with Adversaries

The Amiga, as her name suggests, is the most likable of the archetypes—the quintessential girlfriend. You'd be wrong, though, to see her as weak or fluffy, just a chick out for a good time. Like Savitri, she is a mistress of alliances: willing to walk alongside angel or devil alike if it will serve her cause.

Sabrina is a young woman I know, a PhD candidate at a large Midwestern university, who takes the Amiga's approach. Her department, as is typical of academic departments, is divided into two factions, each hostile toward the other. One faction, call them the theorists, comprises the faculty and graduate students who dive deep into the history of the field, using qualitative research methods to probe its foundations, reinterpret timeless questions, and reshape theoretical frameworks. The other faction, call them the practitioners, emphasizes experiment, quantitative analysis, and practical research that aims to provide workable solutions to current problems. The theorists look down on the practitioners as mere number crunchers, cookbook followers lacking broad vision and creative intellect; the practitioners, in turn, scorn the theorists as arrogant navel-gazers whose work has no relevance to the real world.

Sabrina, though primarily a theorist, has interests that span both factions. When she entered the program she declared to her adviser her intent to act as a bridge, even a peacemaker, between the two camps, which her adviser thought a fine idea; after all, in graduate school (as in life), the more people who'll speak well of you, the better off you are when it comes time to find a job. But in Sabrina's first week, at an evening get-together for women in the department, she found herself wondering if that sort of outreach was even worth trying. After chatting pleasantly for a while with three or four other attendees, she mentioned that her focus was theory, whereupon one woman rolled her eyes and said, "Oh my god. You're one of *them*"—then turned on her heel and walked away.

Sabrina decided to avoid such events for a while and redirect her efforts toward the professors in the practitioner camp.

One such faculty member was a Professor MacFinn, who taught a course called Review of Methods. Required of all first-year doctoral students, the class was primarily practical, consisting of an overview of the field's several subfields and the research methods used in each. It assumed a working knowledge of statistics and data analysis, which Sabrina lacked, but she had heard from the second- and third-year grad students that she needn't worry: Professor MacFinn was lenient toward the theorists, allowing them to adapt the course assignments in favor of qualitative studies and to skip the quantitative, experiment-oriented content. "Just tell him you want to write five theory papers," said one third-year, with a dismissive shrug. "That's what *we* all did. MacFinn doesn't care."

Sabrina said nothing. She suspected, however, that MacFinn did care—probably quite a lot. She went to his office hours the next day.

"Welcome to the program," MacFinn said, motioning to the chair by his desk. "Your first field is theory, correct?" He was in his early 60s, a typically rumpled academic with tortoiseshell-rimmed glasses and a full head of woolly gray hair.

"Yes, Professor," Sabrina said, taking a seat. "I'll be in your Review of Methods class, and I had a few concerns I wanted to discuss. You see—"

He cut her off with a hand wave. "Of course, of course. I'm fine with theorists taking their own path through the class." His tone was tired, resigned. "The department chair has made it clear that's allowable. So don't worry, you can do it your way." He glanced at his laptop screen, then at the door, as if hoping she'd leave now. "All set, then?"

Sabrina took a breath. "No, that's just it, Professor. I want to do it the regular way."

He looked back at her, eyebrows scrunched. "What?"

"I want to do the class the normal way. Follow the whole syllabus. Do all the practical assignments. Would that be all right? Because I feel I need to learn that whole side of the field, not just because I'll need it to get a job but because I think it's interesting and important. I think the best theorists are also practitioners"—she smiled—"and vice versa. So I want to get a complete grounding."

MacFinn scratched his temple. "You're saying you want to do the whole class. In its standard form." His brows scrunched even more.

"That's right. But the thing is: I'm going to need help, because I don't have a strong background in quantitative methods, let alone statistics. So I also wanted to ask if you'd give me the extra coaching. I know it's an imposition."

He stared at her for a moment longer, as if still uncomprehending. Then his face relaxed; he leaned forward. "Of course! Of course! Absolutely! I'm happy to help. We can meet weekly, or just when you feel you need it. Whatever works for you. I'll be delighted." He was beaming. "The best theorists are also practitioners—and vice versa. That's very well said." He chuckled, tapping his palm on the desk. "Yes, very well said."

Sabrina thanked him profusely. MacFinn proceeded to ask her about her interests in the field and plans for study, giving her an opportunity to talk about the many things she appreciated about the practical subfields and the many links she saw between them and theory. He allowed as how he, too, saw those links. "Although, I'm afraid there are some in the department who do not," he said, shaking his head regretfully. At the end of the conversation, he walked Sabrina to the door, thanked her for coming, and reiterated how much he was looking forward to having her in class.

With MacFinn's help, she aced the course.

The next semester she had her eye on an advanced-level practical class that, ordinarily, would be off-limits to a first-year theory student. She went to the professor and, taking the same tack she had with MacFinn, presented her case: stated her eagerness to attend, explained the course's relevance to her core interests, acknowledged she didn't have the prerequisites, and asked if it would nevertheless be all right for her to enroll—and if so, could she get the help she needed? The professor (a woman this time) was just as amenable as MacFinn had been, and happy to assist. Once again, Sabrina got top marks.

Mind you, none of this came easily. Sabrina couldn't just skate through; she had to show herself willing to put in the work, or else the professors would have seen that her claim of interest in the practical subfields was merely a sham. But she did put in the work. With her former adversaries, she walked the path from start to finish, paying them due respect and gaining their respect in turn. In giving them her trust, she received their trust. What a contrast with the other theory students, whose approach to the same problem was to plead to be excused; and how could the professors not feel refreshed by Sabrina's very different approach? "Like as water to a thirsty man, so are these words you utter," says Yama. "Therefore my faith in you is supreme."

Learning from the Amiga

There's a lot that could be said about being the Amiga, but I'll focus on the one big thing she knows that most of us do not. She knows that **relationships exist in two dimensions**, not one.

Most of us see our relationships as falling along a continuum from *friend* to *foe*. If I get along well with someone—a colleague, say, who's easy to work with and a pleasant lunch companion—I label him a friend, or perhaps a casual friend. But that other guy, the one who's always so rude and difficult—well, if he isn't exactly a foe, he's certainly no friend.

This view is inadequate. As Laurence Stybel and Maryanne Peabody write in an article for *MIT Sloan Management Review*, relationships should be arrayed along not one but two dimensions: whether the person is *with* us or *against* us, and whether that stance is *conditional* or *unconditional*. Combined, these two dimensions give us four main relationship types: friends, foes, allies, and adversaries (see figure 2).[2]

Friends are unconditionally with you, foes unconditionally against you. A friend is someone with whom you share a bond of love or duty; someone who will support you no matter what. A foe is someone who regards you with personal, deep-rooted antagonism; someone who will oppose you no matter what. Allies and adversaries, on the other hand, support or oppose you when and because it suits them: allies supporting you based on (currently) shared interests, adversaries opposing you based on (currently) conflicting interests. Allies and adversaries may convert, one to the other, depending on whether their interests come into or fall out of alignment with yours. In other words, the line between ally and adversary is thin, while the line between friend and foe is thick.

Figure 2: Relationship Types

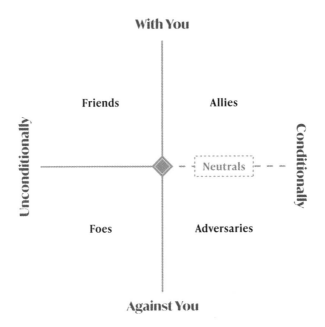

Of course, this doesn't mean we can't lose friends. A friend might hurt or disappoint us, or we them, and we might part ways or even become foes as a result. There are also such things as frenemies: people entwined in love-hate relationships. The point is not that friendship is always pure and eternal, but rather that friends are attached by durable bonds while allies are attached by flexible links. Moreover, while true friendships are wonderful, they're scarce and, let's be honest, take a lot of time and effort. Alliances, in contrast, are abundant in their potential, useful, and, though not maintenance-free, relatively easy to forge. We saw how Princess Savitri made a most improbable ally during a brief walk in the woods.

The Amiga knows the first step in cultivating fruitful alliances is to stop expecting one's allies to be one's friends. Imagine a colleague who supports you staunchly until there comes a day when supporting you means she risks losing her job. If she turns her back on you then, what will your reaction be? If you saw her as a friend you might blame her, but blaming an ally for not being a friend is painful and pointless. Instead, we should appreciate the part allies play in our life and strive, whenever possible, to keep our interests aligned with theirs.

More good news: Some, perhaps even most, of your supposed enemies are actually just adversaries, available for flipping. Show them how your interests align—as Sabrina did with Professor MacFinn—and bam, you've got yourself a new ally. Even better, it's often the case that an adversary is making an unfounded assumption that puts the two of you at odds; dispel that assumption, and the hostility melts away. MacFinn assumed Sabrina was like all the other theory students he'd encountered: just another snotty grad student looking for a way to blow off his class. As soon as she showed him he was wrong, he became her eager supporter. And again, consider Savitri: when Yama showed up, she might have assumed he was (literally) a lethal enemy and assailed him with tears or curses. Instead, she overturned *his* assumption—that every mortal hates and fears him—by becoming a fellow walker and talker.

How does the Amiga do it? There are hundreds of self-help books (mostly categorized under negotiation or sales skills) that teach alliance-making. Among the techniques you'll find in such books are the following:

- Signal your desire to work together rather than compete.
- Think in terms of interests ("We both want this project to succeed") rather than positions ("I need at least 70 percent of the budget").
- Seek to understand your adversaries' preferences, values, and assumptions, and be open about your own.
- Emphasize points of reconciliation and alignment rather than differences.
- Early in a dispute, find a point on which you can agree.

In my experience, though, lack of skill isn't usually the problem. We all know what's required in order to build a better relationship with someone: talk with them, listen to them, share our thoughts and feelings, seek to understand theirs. None of this is rocket science. What's hard, very hard, is to make the initial shift in perspective *from* "He's an enemy; I wonder how to get the best of him?" *to* "He and I are at odds; I wonder how we might become better aligned?"

In an episode of the television series *Downton Abbey*, there's a scene in which Cora, Countess of Grantham, tries to enlist her mother-in-law, the Dowager Countess, in an effort to protect a particular family interest. The two women haven't always seen eye to eye. When the Dowager indicates her willingness to help, Cora sighs with relief and says, "So we're friends?" The Dowager replies: "*Allies*, my dear, which are far more useful."

The Amiga—despite her friendly moniker—would agree.

6

THE MESMERIST

ONCE UPON A TIME THERE was a king who loved his wife more than anything in the world. Secure in her love and fidelity, he thought himself the happiest of men. Then one day it was revealed to him that not only was she unfaithful, she was deceiving him with his greatest enemy, with whom she was plotting to assassinate him and take the throne. At first he refused to believe it, but his loyal vizier assured him it was true. Mad with grief and rage, he ordered the queen's execution. Then he vowed that each day henceforth he would select a maiden of his kingdom to marry, take her to his bed that night, and in the morning, have her head chopped off. "Thus," he said, "I will make sure I am never again deceived by a woman."

For a few years the king followed this evil policy, and no arguments or beseeching from his advisers could turn him from his course. Every parent in the land lived in terror that their daughter would be the next one chosen. Beheading followed beheading. At last the king's vizier came to him with the news that there were no more maidens available.

"I don't want to hear it!" shouted the king. "Don't *you* have two daughters of marriageable age? Bring me one of them! If you don't, I'll have you and your entire family put to death."

Now it was the vizier's turn to be terrified. Home he went and, trembling, informed his daughters what the king had said. "I won't do it," he assured them.

"Papa, you must," said the elder daughter. Her name was Shahrazade. She was a beautiful and brilliant girl with a passion for books of all kinds: she had read hundreds of stories and loved to amuse her younger sister, Dunyazad, by retelling them.

"The king will kill you! I can't bear it," said the vizier, tears washing his cheeks.

"We have no choice, Papa," said Shahrazade. Her face was grave but calm as she kissed him. "I must go. But be of good hope! I intend to be alive in the morning."[1]

Shahrazade: Mind-Changer

The two hundred separate stories of *The Thousand and One Nights* (sometimes called *The Arabian Nights*) were written over a period from the twelfth to the sixteenth century and first appeared outside the Islamic world, translated into French, between 1704 and 1712. Translations into other European languages soon followed. There is not and never was a definitive version; the stories come from a long and multifarious oral tradition, and many of the ones popularized by Western media, such as "Sinbad the Sailor" and "Aladdin and the Wonderful Lamp," were late additions to the collection. Present and consistent across all versions, however, is the famous frame story, in which Shahrazad—known in the West as Scheherazade—beguiles her murderous husband with a series of wondrous tales, thereby causing him to postpone her death night after night, for one thousand and one nights, until he finally relents and takes her to his heart.

The Mesmerist, like our other two earth-water archetypes (Mama Bear and

Amiga), is mistress of the indirect approach. Trickery, some call it, to which I say: Yes, indeed. Women have always needed to resort to trickery–not merely in order to get what they want, but to survive in a world in which men hold most of the authority; a world in which the whim of one's husband-master, backed by the law's apparatus and society's approval, can result in terrible injury, up to and including death. No literary character better illustrates this dire need for subterfuge, and woman's consequent skill at influencing obliquely, than Shahrazad.

To return to the story: Shahrazad's father the vizier is nearly dead with grief, but she finally persuades him to let her go to the king, assuring him she has a plan–though she will not say what it is. She asks that her sister, Dunyazad, be allowed to accompany her. The vizier reluctantly agrees. *So I will lose both my daughters*, he thinks. *But what can I do?**

The wedding occurs. The next morning, Shahrazad and the king wake before first light. Shahrazad has asked permission for her sister to come see her, ostensibly to say goodbye, but she has given Dunyazad secret instructions:

> An hour before the dawn you must come in as if you meant to take leave of me. But you must not do so immediately. Instead you must present a cup of delicious sherbet to the King and another cup to me. Then I want you to say: "Tell me, I beg you, as you have so often done, some strange story, so that we may the better enjoy the cool hour before the sun reddens the sky!" Do not fail in this, dear sister, for our lives may depend upon it![2]

As promised, Dunyazad comes with the cups of cool sherbet and asks Shahrazad for a story. The king, feeling restless, is pleased with the idea and gives his consent.

Shahrazad begins a tale about a merchant traveling in a foreign land who sits down to rest under a shade tree in a garden, there to eat some bread and

---

* In some versions of the story, it is the vizier himself who must perform the executions. We can imagine the terror and despair he must have felt, knowing that soon he would be forced to kill both his daughters.

dates. He throws away a date stone, inadvertently striking the jinn (or genie) of the garden in the chest. The enraged jinn appears in a boil of smoke and declares the offender must die. The unhappy man begs for a year in which to set his affairs in order. "All right," says the jinn, "on condition you swear to return to the same spot one year hence to meet your fate." One year to the day the merchant does return, and . . .

But there Shahrazad breaks off, saying with a sigh that there is no time for more. The sun is rising and the king must go to court, for he has much to do.

"But what happened to the unfortunate merchant?" asks her sister.

"Ah!" says Shahrazad. "The things that happened were very strange! Indeed the next part is much more exciting, and I would gladly tell it, if only I had time."[3]

"By Allah," says the king, "I, too, would like to know what happens next."

"Tomorrow, if the King spare me," Shahrazad replies, "I will tell the rest." And the king, deciding he can just as well have her executed tomorrow, departs for the court.

Before sunrise next morning, Dunyazad arrives with the sherbet and Shahrazade continues the narrative of the merchant and the jinn, this time weaving in another tale, a sub-story if you will, about two men: one whose wife has been turned into a gazelle, another whose two brothers have been turned into black dogs. These men show up just as the merchant has returned to the garden to await his appointment with death. The jinn appears and is curious; the men offer to tell him their strange history—if he'll spare the merchant's life. "I agree," says the jinn, "but only if I like what I hear." Thus Shahrazade launches into another marvelous tale, only to arrive at the most suspenseful part just as dawn is breaking. Once again, the king decides he must hear the rest. "I can always kill her tomorrow," he thinks, as he heads for the throne room.

And on she goes: night after night after night.

To **leave them wanting more** is job one for a Mesmerist. Finish the story, and no matter how good it was, your audience will soon be browsing other volumes. End the show, and even if you get a standing ovation, in a minute they'll be shuffling up the aisles trying to remember where they parked. Of course in real life, every party must come to an end (*and thank goodness for that*, say most of us); the Mesmerist, however, knows to leave her fellow partygoers—whether friends, colleagues, or clients—eagerly anticipating something yet to come. In sales training programs one learns never to end a call without gaining agreement to a next step, for to hang up the phone without such agreement is to risk losing the customer's interest. Looking to another type of sales: Gypsy Rose Lee, the famous stripper of the post-vaudeville era, had a stock line she included in her act: "My mother always told me to make them beg for more, and then—don't give it to them!" It might as well be the Mesmerist's motto.

For a thousand and one nights, Shahrazad weaves her stories. Sometimes she nests them together, one inside the other like Russian dolls, so that the king can only be sure of hearing what happens in the main story if he listens to several sub-stories first. Other times she contrives to reach a cliffhanger just as the sun is rising. Each morning, the king goes off to court declaring he can't rest until he knows what happens next, and each morning, he decides to put off his wife's death another day.

It's hard to imagine having the patience and stamina required to keep this up—for three years! But **extraordinary persistence** is another hallmark of the Mesmerist. More than any of her sister archetypes, she plays the long game. We've seen how the Amiga, an expert at showing how existing interests align, can flip an adversary to an ally in a matter of minutes, while the Mama Bear, who hand-selects eager "kids" for her audience, can be equally quick to charm. For their work, Amiga and Mama Bear seek out fertile ground—or at least, ground that needs only a bit of water and some judicious weeding to bring forth fruit, often in short order. The Mesmerist, on the other hand, is out to achieve something much more toilsome, much more audacious: she is out to transform deserts into gardens. To make a desert bloom is not a short-term project. Shahrazad knows she must keep the king enthralled not for one night, not for seven nights, but for a thousand nights: that's how long it will take for his madness to abate, allowing him to enter a new state of mind in which he might reconsider his hateful vow.

If you think this all sounds like the work of a guru, you have put your finger on a third quality of the Mesmerist: she **aims to enlighten**. In an interview for *The Atlantic*, scholar and author Hanan al-Shaykh discusses Shahrazade's brilliance as a teacher:

> Shahrazad's power over the king does not stop with her ability to keep herself alive by entertaining him. Ultimately, she exerts far more power over him than that. Though the *Arabian Nights* feature countless characters and voices, we must read each one as partially channeled by Shahrazad, her plea for reason and mercy. Through all these stories she is working on him. Educating him. Maybe she is brainwashing him. These stories, in fact, slowly teach him to give up his lust for blood and his blanket condemnation of women.[4]

Al-Shaykh notes that there is a progression in the stories. At first, Shahrazade tells of ordinary men and women who find themselves threatened by evil jinns, sorcerers, or tyrants and consequently must cajole or connive their way out of danger—tales designed to arouse sympathy for the oppressed. As she goes on, new themes emerge, featuring people facing difficult decisions: Should I punish my lying slave? Is it wrong to steal from thieves? May I kill my tormentor even if he's old and weak? Gradually, the moral questions the stories raise become more complex. Next, Shahrazad introduces a new main character, one based on a historical ruler who loved art and poetry and believed in equality among his subjects: Haroun al-Rashid, who, it is said, used to disguise himself as a poor man and roam the streets to check on his people's well-being. Once, upon learning of the murder of a young woman of the city, Haroun issued this statement: "I want you to find her killer. I want to avenge this girl. How else can I stand before my God and Creator on judgment day?"[5] Haroun is the opposite of Shahrazade's vengeful husband, and as he grows more prominent in her narrative he provides a model for a different type of king: wise, tolerant, and humane. Thus Shahrazade leads her would-be executioner, step by slow step, toward enlightenment; to save herself, yes, but also to save him.

On the thousand and first night, she finishes her story just as the sun rises.

There is no time to begin another. Dunyazad, alarmed but seeing her sister smile, says nothing. After a short silence, Shahrazad speaks: "For a thousand nights, O King, I have whiled away the hour before the dawn with some tale of adventure or pleasure ... Have I yet—have I, in all this time—found favor in the eyes of the King?"[6]

At her words the king hangs his head in shame. Shahrazad waits, then takes his hand and says gently: "Allah does not demand from his servants the fulfillment of an evil vow, O King."

And the king, shedding a tear, replies:

> O most beloved of Queens, it has long been impossible for me to fulfill that evil vow! For in truth I have long known that you are the most excellent of women, the best of wives, and the light of my eyes! I have long bitterly regretted my former cruelty and wickedness ... and all by reason of your excellence. How can I reward you?[7]

But the Mesmerist asks no reward—other than the reward of knowing that with her persistent magic, she changed a mind for the better.

Cheryl: Sole Member of the Five Million Dollar Club

At our company's annual all-hands meeting, awards would be presented to employees for various achievements. One category of awards was for sales-people: there was a Rookie of the Year award for the best new recruit and an Account Director of the Year award for the best all-round sales professional. Then there were the so-called clubs, which celebrated those who had brought in a certain amount of revenue over the course of the year. The Million Dollar Club always had nine or ten members; the Two Million Dollar Club, three or four. The names would be called out by our CEO, and one by one the recipients would come up and join the line on stage, there to be applauded and handed their plaques.

There was rarely a Three Million Dollar Club, never a Four Million Dollar

Club. But there was always a Five Million Dollar Club. And of that club, there was only ever one member. Her name was Cheryl.

Cheryl had a warm manner and a wide smile. She dressed well, though not as glamorously as some of the other women account directors; she favored plain skirt- or pantsuits with low heels and a silk scarf. Though average in height and frame, she was athletic; she and her husband played doubles tennis competitively, in later years winning medals at the Senior Olympics. She had joined the company in the early 1980s and retired in 2020, making her tenure there something close to four decades.

Cheryl was the force behind another component of the annual meeting: the Follies, a (very) amateur and (very) light-hearted production featuring songs, skits, and parodies by employees. A couple weeks before the event, just when everyone was thinking, "I guess there won't be a Follies this year," Cheryl would spring into action. She would send out the call for skits (no submission was ever rejected), put the program together, hound reluctant folks to participate, and generally whip up enthusiasm for this long-standing company tradition. Then on show night, she would serve as emcee as well as lead the opening number, which wasn't a parody but rather an encomium to the firm and its people, the lyrics written by Cheryl and (for some reason I never understood) set to the tune of "California, Here I Come."

But besides her showmanship, the most notable thing about Cheryl was her selling ability. No one, and I mean no one, at the company ever closed more or larger deals than she. Year after year, she was the sole member of the Five, sometimes it was Six, Million Dollar Club. And the odd thing was, nobody could quite explain how she did it.

"In performance management," said a colleague of mine who was with the company for much of Cheryl's time there, "you get evaluated on the *what* and the *how*. Cheryl certainly had the *what*—her results were undeniable—but I never got the *how*. She was so draining!"

It wasn't just her coworkers whom she drained. A project manager who worked with her told me that clients, too, could find her annoying, once going so far as to say they wanted her off their team. Was she too pushy, like Lacey, our Amazon of chapter 2? No. Cheryl was a model of consultative selling. Although she was certainly confident, she would never have pulled a Lacey and told a client, "We're not doing that." On the contrary: she was ever polite, ever the listener, ever striving to build relationships. Nevertheless, she got on people's nerves.

So why was she so successful?

The answer that comes up again and again is: She was *persistent*.

"She was like a dog with a bone," said the project manager. "She would get a nibble and just go after it: find the right people, the right relationships."

"Whenever she called," said my colleague, "my first thought was, *This is going to be a grind.* With other account directors, you could usually give them a little guidance and send them on their way. With Cheryl, you were trapped. There was no escape."

I remember the feeling well: the phone would ring, I'd look at caller ID, see it was Cheryl, and my heart would sink. I knew she would have something creative in mind for one of her big clients, and that she was looking for a consultant (me) to put together the proposal for her. Cheryl liked to push the envelope; unlike other salespeople, who tended to rely on our standard products and, at most, mix and match various components thereof, she relished the challenge and prestige of devising something brand new. Our products were corporate training programs—workshops, seminars, online learning—and although profit margins were much better on the off-the-shelf stuff, customized programs (or "bespoke" programs, to use the British term) had always been our company's strength. As long as a salesperson could get a consultant to design the thing, there were no limits on how innovative we could get. And Cheryl loved to be innovative.

There was a process the account directors were supposed to follow if they needed help with business development. Cheryl invariably went around that process. She would decide whom she wanted help from, call that person directly, and refuse to take "No" for an answer. You might suggest she call Resourcing; she'd say you were clearly the best person for this gig, so there was no need to go through Resourcing. You'd point her to some clients where we'd done something similar before, which she could use as models; she'd say great, thanks, and could you please include those examples in the proposal you'd be putting together? You'd say you had only half a day to work on it; she'd say no problem, it surely wouldn't take longer than that.

Throughout the conversation she would be supremely pleasant: thanking you, praising your abilities, asking nicely, never the least bit ruffled. She never talked about what *she* wanted; it was always about the Very Important Client and what *they* wanted. How could you say no to a Very Important Client? You found yourself being carried along, saying "OK, yes, sure," while inside you were screaming, "Don't wanna!" It really was like being mesmerized.

And in the end, with the proposal complete, the pitch made, and the deal sealed (as it almost invariably was), you felt . . . good. You had pushed yourself. You had done something big. You were on the winning team. As my colleague put it:

> If you were willing to go outside your comfort zone with her, there was a lot to be gained. The times I did that, I learned a lot. Because she grated on me, I resisted her. But if I had it to do over again, I would spend more time going with her rather than resisting her. As the person who made *her* successful, *I* would have been more successful.

> She was like the coach who knows how to get more from you than you thought you could give or even wanted to give. You look back and think, *What a pain! But that coach got more effort and talent out of me than I believed possible. Higher levels than I ever thought I could achieve.*

My friend the project manager echoed that thought: "Every day, she would get me to do stuff I didn't want to do. I would begrudgingly do it, and in the end, it would turn out to be a good thing. Why did I resist every time? If I hadn't, it might have been better."

The Mesmerist is among the most optimistic of the archetypes: for her there is no "No" that can't be turned into a "Yes," no antagonist so intractable they can't be brought round. All one has to do is keep at it. A Mesmerist like Shahrazad or Cheryl has the ability to look beyond what a person thinks they want or don't want, need or don't need, and see their potential for a higher good. Resistance, complaints, even threats will not deter her.

Salespeople are taught to handle objections by encouraging the customer to "say more" and then listening hard so that, eventually, they can provide a useful and relevant response. Cheryl didn't do that. For her, objections simply didn't exist. When you said "can't" or "won't," it was as though she hadn't heard you. "I understand," she'd say. "Now, the most exciting thing about this client situation is ..."

And on she'd go, weaving the story and inviting you in.

Learning from the Mesmerist

You might imagine that to be a Mesmerist, you must be an expert story-teller, like Shahrazade, or an expert salesperson, like Cheryl. Although that might help, this archetype's power really depends on three traits that are more mundane.

Persist ... nicely. We've seen how Cheryl "nagged" her targets until she got what she wanted. But she wasn't nasty about it. "She would never chew you out," said my colleague. "She was persistent, but she did it with a smile." Sheryl Sandberg, author of *Lean In*,* talks about how women can find the right balance of nagging and nice when it comes to negotiating salaries:

> Just being nice is not a winning strategy. Nice sends a message that the woman is willing to sacrifice pay to be liked by others. This is why a woman needs to combine niceness with insistence, a style that Mary Sue Coleman, president of the University of Michigan, calls

---

* See the opening chapter for more about Sandberg's theories of women's empowerment.

"relentlessly pleasant." This method requires smiling frequently, expressing appreciation and concern, invoking common interests, emphasizing larger goals, and approaching the negotiation as solving a problem as opposed to taking a critical stance.[8]

The Mesmerist applies "relentlessly pleasant" to much more than salary negotiations. It's her modus operandi. Shahrazad was both relentless and pleasant with her husband the king; remember how she orchestrated each morning's storytelling session, having her sister arrive with the tasty sherbet and ask for a story, thereby signaling not stressful entreaties, but a delightful interlude for the king to enjoy before the start of his workday. In the same way (though in far less fraught circumstances), Cheryl would orchestrate the conversation with you, her audience of one, to feel not like a pressured harangue, but like a flattering invitation to participate on the winning team in an interesting new game—one that would yield prizes all round.

What does "relentlessly pleasant" look like? Mary Sue Coleman, quoted above, has it right: Smile frequently. Express appreciation and concern. Invoke common interests. Eschew criticism. And . . .

Emphasize larger goals. Everyone I spoke with about Cheryl agrees: her number one concern was always the client. You never felt she was out for herself. It was always about meeting the client's needs, providing them with a solution that was new and effective. She pushed hard for the client's sake. Shahrazade, of course, wants to forestall her execution, but it isn't only that; she also wants to the king to grow in wisdom, compassion, and humanity, so that he'll forsake his murderous vow. After all, if all she did was prevent her own death—say the king decided to make her his senior wife and spare her life, but go on taking concubines as his daily victims—that wouldn't be any good. She has to change his mind and heart entirely: to create, if you will, a garden from a desert. The Mesmerist is never just an entertainer. She is an educator, an inspirer, a transformer.*

---

* I should also note that in some versions, the king dies soon after promising to keep Shahrazad as his queen, and an unnamed "good king" takes the throne. In an essay

And transformation takes time. Maybe there's a difficult colleague, call him Mark, with whom you have to work on a long-term project. You can't avoid him, and your initial efforts to find common ground have been unsuccessful. The truth is, Mark is obnoxious—one of those men whose swagger and competitiveness conceals deep insecurities—and the two of you really are at odds. *All right*, you think; *I'll play the long game.* You greet Mark every day with a smile. No matter how he behaves, you continue unflustered. If he shouts, you respond cordially. If he accuses you of undermining him, you assure him you would never do that and change the subject to the task at hand. You ask his advice and listen with interest. You thank him for his insights. And at every turn, you bring the conversation back to the larger goals to which both of you are—you relentlessly assume—dedicated. It may take six weeks, it may take six months, but rest assured: in the end, Mark's going to come around.

Give your audience space. Shahrazade had a talent for breaking off just at the most exciting part of the story, but the real-life Mesmerist need not have that talent. What she does need is an inclination for giving her audience space: space to react, to respond, to participate in the show. "Engage through involvement" was a precept in one of the sales training programs offered by my former company, and engaging through involvement is really what the Mesmerist is doing when she leaves them wanting more. When the king leans forward and says, "But what happened to the unfortunate merchant?" it's because Shahrazade has drawn him into a scenario, and then—stopped. The morning quiet opens up like a vessel, inviting the king to fill it with his own thoughts, his own anticipation and wonder. It's not what the Mesmerist says that matters most; it's what she does not say. A vacuum is one of the most powerful forces there is. It *will* be filled. If you don't fill it, your audience will.

So, if you would be a Mesmerist, try saying less. Prepare your presentation,

---

in the *New York Times* on May 30, 2021, author Salman Rushdie theorizes that the king dies at the hands of his wife and her sister and that the new "good king" is their father, the former vizier. Perhaps Shahrazad has more of the Empress and Witch in her than I thought!

then replace your conclusion—the one where you tie everything up with a ribbon, offering your brilliant recommendations and solutions—with a question. The question should be some version of "What do you think?" (*Not* "Do you agree?") Better yet, replace half your content with questions: open-ended ones that invite your audience to chime in along the way. You may worry they'll fail to grasp your point. That's OK. People don't care about grasping your point; they want to be part of the story.

There's an old saying sometimes attributed to Benjamin Franklin: "Tell me and I forget, teach me and I may remember, involve me and I learn." The Mesmerist involves us, and we learn. Sometimes, we are even transformed.

PART THREE

WATER-AIR

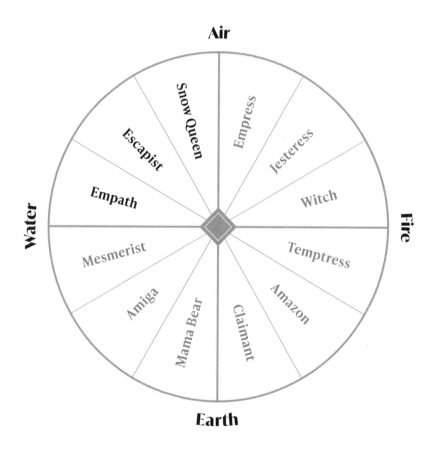

7

THE EMPATH

ANOTHER KING, ANOTHER PROBLEM.

This king's name was Zhuang, and he lived in China, two hundred *li* to the south of Mount Song.[1] He had a consort and three daughters, but the youngest daughter, Miaoshan, he'd banished years ago because she had refused to marry, insisting instead on becoming a nun.

Now King Zhuang was very sick—with jaundice, which had spread all over his skin and throughout his body. He could neither sleep nor eat. As is usual in such stories, he had summoned the best doctors in the land, but none could cure him.

He had been suffering for three years when one day there arrived at the palace a monk who claimed to know of a divine remedy to cure the illness. "This remedy requires two ingredients," the monk said. "It requires the hands and eyes of one without anger."[2]

"Ridiculous!" said the king. "If I take someone's hands and eyes, obviously he'll be angry." But the monk said such a person did exist: a hermit, living on a mountain not far away. "This person has no anger," he said. "If you can get the hands and eyes, you'll be cured."

Hearing this, the king offered up a prayer: "May this hermit bestow upon me hands and eyes without stint or grudge." He sent an envoy to go ask.

Off went the envoy to the hermit's abode. He bowed and presented the king's request. The hermit at once agreed, saying only: "I shall give my hands and eyes to provide medicine for him. My one desire is that the remedy may match the ailment and will drive out the king's disease. The king must direct his mind toward enlightenment ... then he will achieve recovery."[3]

With that, the hermit gouged out both eyes with a knife. The hermit then gave the knife to the envoy, and the envoy severed the hermit's hands. After promising to remember what the hermit had said, the envoy took the items and returned to the palace.

The monk blended the medicine, which the king took. Within ten days, he was cured.

Astounded by his good fortune, the king vowed to go to the mountain and make thank-offerings to the hermit. Taking his consort, his two daughters, and a large retinue, he made the journey and, upon reaching the simple hut, laid out the finest gifts and delivered a formal speech of gratitude. But his consort, who had been looking closely at the blind, mutilated figure seated there, began to cry and said to the king: "When I look at the hermit ... I don't know ... she is very like our daughter Miaoshan."

And the hermit suddenly spoke: "My lady mother! Do not cast your mind back to Miaoshan. I am she. When my father the king suffered the foul disease, your child offered up her hands and eyes to repay the king's love."

The king, overcome with grief and remorse, embraced his daughter and prayed that her eyes and hands might be restored.* But all at once Miaoshan disappeared, and ...

---

* The similarities between the Miaoshan story and Shakespeare's *King Lear* have caused scholars to wonder if there is a common textual source, but no such link has been found. I believe, however, that we have here an excellent example of an archetypal tale: one that recurs again and again across gulfs of time and culture. See the final chapter, "The Master Maid," for another example of such a tale.

…heaven and earth shook, radiance blazed forth, auspicious clouds enclosed all about, heavenly drums resounded. And then was seen the All-Compassionate Guanyin of the Thousand Hands and Thousand Eyes, solemn and majestic in form, radiant with dazzling light, lofty and magnificent like the moon amid the stars.[4]

Guanyin: The Sounds of Suffering

Suppose you discovered the secret to perfect happiness. Knowing this secret, you could withdraw from the world, ascend to a higher plane and dwell there, experiencing ineffable joy, wanting for nothing, free from all suffering forever.

Would you take that deal?

Many of us would in a second. But a bodhisattva—a Buddhist saint—makes a different choice. Having achieved a state of enlightenment, he or she opts to stay involved (perhaps in supernatural form) in the messy world in order to help others achieve enlightenment as well. Bodhisattvas are teacher-angels, forgoing their own bliss so that they might instruct and elevate the rest of us. The most revered of all the bodhisattvas is Guanyin.

Her name is short for Guanshiyin, which in Chinese means "The One Who Perceives the Sounds of the World." The sounds are those of suffering: the cries of sickness, pain, hunger, fear, delusion, and despair that arise in a dull roar from every corner of the earth, 24 hours a day, 365 days a year. Guanyin's thousand eyes see every misfortune; her thousand hands reach out to help all who ask her aid.* Her shrines abound throughout the Buddhist world, visited by pilgrims who come in faith that she and she alone will hear their prayers, cure their afflictions, and alleviate their misery. Outside China she is known by other names, but her nature is the same everywhere. She is the All-Compassionate: the paradigm of the Empath.

---

* You'd think The One Who Perceives the Sounds of the World would have a thousand ears rather than a thousand eyes. But I suppose her two ears, exquisitely attuned, are somehow enough.

Her worship predates the story of Miaoshan by many generations, although her representations prior to the tenth century CE were almost always masculine. In the Lotus Sutra, believed to have been composed in the first century, s/he is known as Avalokiteshvara and is of fluid gender. By the twelfth century, she was generally interpreted as female. In today's China, she is often depicted as a beautiful young woman in a white robe.

The Miaoshan story (according to Glen Dudbridge, author of the most extensive study of the legend) originated almost a thousand years ago at the Xiangshan monastery, located in Henan Province in central China. Near the monastery there stood a sacred building known as the All-Compassionate Pagoda. It is said to have once housed a statue of the Bodhisattva Guanyin with 36 arms and, in the palms of her hands, 36 eyes. The statue disappeared at some time in the distant past, but the pagoda still stands.

In the year 1100, the abbot of Xiangshan monastery invited the prefect of a nearby city, a man named Jiang Zhiqi, to pay him a visit. The abbot told Prefect Jiang a story about a monk in tattered robes who had arrived at the monastery one day a few months earlier, bearing a book-scroll entitled *The Life of the All-Compassionate Bodhisattva of Xiangshan*. The monk said the words were those of a divine spirit, communicated directly to a certain Zen master, and that they recounted how the bodhisattva Guanyin had taken on human form and had later achieved enlightenment right there in the district of Xiangshan. The abbot asked for permission to make a copy, which the monk allowed.

Having explained the book's existence, the abbot gave it to Prefect Jiang to read. Jiang, in his account, says he found the language "occasionally vulgar," but the bodhisattva's own words "quite unique—utterances that penetrated the deepest truth."[5] The bodhisattva had been a princess named Miaoshan. Jiang inscribed the story (making, he said, some improvements) on a stone tablet, copies of which spread throughout China and have come down to us today.

There seems little doubt that the original tale was cooked up by the abbot and/or the prefect in a bid to increase the flow of pilgrim-tourists to the area; nevertheless, the legend took hold of the imaginations of Buddhists everywhere and went on to inspire popular versions by many other authors. (I especially like it because it gives the lie to the common belief that male writers and artists of the past thought about women only in conventional terms; here we have a monastery abbot and a city administrator, surely the stodgiest of types, claiming that the most magnificent bodhisattva of them all made her earthly appearance in female form.)

Guanyin, in both her embodied and her transfigured form, represents the Empath archetype in several ways. The first is implicit in her name: "The One Who Hears the Sounds of the (Suffering) World." When the young Miaoshan's parents tell her she must marry—her father even cutting off her food and water in an effort to starve her into submission—she replies that she will do so only if it prevents three misfortunes. Her mother asks what she means. She replies:

> The first is this: when the men of this world are young their face is as fair as the jade-like moon, but when old age comes their hair turns white, their face is wrinkled, in motion or repose they are in every way worse off than in their youth. The second is this: a man's limbs may be lusty and vigorous ... but when once an illness befalls him he lies in bed without a single pleasure in life. The third is this: a man may have a great assembly of relatives ... but when one day impermanence comes, even such close kin as father or son cannot take his place. If a husband can prevent these three misfortunes, I will marry him. If he cannot, then I vow not to marry. I pity the people of this world, plunged into such suffering ... My purpose is to become a nun in the hope of gaining, through religious discipline, the fulfilment of preventing these great misfortunes on behalf of all mankind.[6]

Old age, illness, and death are the three unavoidable woes of humankind: these sufferings come to us all, no matter our station in life or how hard we try. Of course there is no man who can prevent them, so Miaoshan's promise to marry such a man is rhetorical. Her pity for the people of the world outweighs every other desire. She intends to devote her life to lessening their pain.

I will not delve here into the vast topic of Buddhist thought and its claim that, by following its precepts, suffering can be relieved—indeed, escaped entirely.* I'll just note that the Empath's way begins with **hearing and caring about anguish**, physical and mental. The next step—seeking to alleviate anguish—will look different depending on each Empath's nature. Miaoshan becomes a nun, believing that religious discipline and prayer will be most effective. But her father interferes once again, accusing the nuns of schemes to lure his daughter and threatening their community with extermination if they don't persuade her to return to her family. The nuns, terrified, do their best: "You were born in a royal palace, Miaoshan. Why should you hide away here in a convent? Go home, dear! Marry a prince!"

Miaoshan is unmoved. She proceeds to berate the nuns: "Why is it that you all pursue splendor and extravagance, that your comportment is seductive, your clothing fine and showy? You have irresponsibly entered the Buddhist order... vainly consumed your time."[7]

This tone may seem harsh for an Empath. But Miaoshan, according to the story, has never hesitated to lay it on the line. As a young woman "she never spoke out of turn, and when she did speak it was always to admonish... Those who followed her instruction were all able to convert to goodness."[8]

The Empath should not be mistaken for the warm, feel-good Temptress. She has a cold edge. Like the true friend who cares enough to call out her friend's screw-ups or the good mother who cares enough to discipline her child, the Empath **cares enough to admonish**. Not that she gives people a hard time for the heck of it; her criticism may be tough to hear, but it is purposeful and warranted. And it comes from a place of goodwill. Like the Amazon, the Empath fights for a cause. Her particular cause is to alleviate suffering.

Miaoshan remains in the convent, instructing the nuns and performing

---

* For more on this subject, see my book *The Art of Quiet Influence* (Nicholas Brealey Publishing, 2019). See also *Do You Know Who You Are? Reading the Buddha's Discourses*, by Krishnan Venkatesh (Mercer University Press, 2018).

various miraculous deeds—making a dry spring gush forth, for example, and multiplying the vegetables in the garden—until her father loses his temper completely and decides to execute her for a witch. Miaoshan goes with composure to meet the executioner, but even as the blade swings down she is snatched away by the god of Dragon Mountain, who knows she is about to fulfill her spiritual destiny. After some wandering about, she settles on Fragrant Mountain. There she lives as a hermit, alone and in prayer, until the day the king's envoy comes to ask for her hands and eyes.

Then we see Miaoshan demonstrate a third quality of the Empath: she **begrudges nothing**. For nearly her whole life, her father has treated her with the purest cruelty: threatening her, starving her, and finally trying to kill her. When the god of Dragon Mountain foils that plan, the king goes berserk, sending five hundred soldiers to behead the entire community of nuns and burn down their convent. He says to his consort, Miaoshan's mother: "Do not grieve. This young girl was no kin of mine. She must have been some demon who was born into my family. We have managed to get rid of the demon: that is cause for great delight!"[9]

Then he falls ill, and three years pass before the monk arrives with the strange prescription for a cure. Who could blame Miaoshan if she spat at a royal envoy asking the smallest favor? As for giving up body parts—come on! Remember, although the king has no idea who "the hermit" is, Miaoshan knows full well who the king is and what he has done to her (not to mention to the nuns). Yet she does not hesitate; she gouges out her own eyes before giving the knife to the envoy so he can sever her hands—"to repay the king's love," as she puts it. We might think her life from then on will be a pathetic one, but it turns out her sacrifice is what initiates her transformation into Guanyin: the mighty bodhisattva with the thousand arms and eyes, the All-Compassionate, second only to the Buddha himself. Her father, too, becomes a new man, noble and wise. With vast empathy, it seems, comes vast power.

Nurse Wendy: Bodhisattva of the Psych Ward

In early November 2020, after four months with an undiagnosed neurological disorder that had me suffering from chronic vertigo, anxiety, severe insomnia, nerve pain, more anxiety, more vertigo, worse insomnia, suicidal thoughts, and down and down the spiral went, seemingly unstoppable—I checked myself into the psychiatric ward* of our local hospital.

When at seven p.m. I was admitted, the nurses were in the middle of a change from day to night shift, so although two of them had performed the basics—strip-searched me for drugs and wounds, taken away my backpack and purse for inventorying, checked my vital signs, and shown me my bedroom—they pretty much left me to myself for the first hour. I was in a state of abject terror. *Locked in the asylum*, I kept thinking. *Let me out.* I knew that I was there voluntarily and, by law, could leave as long as I showed I wasn't a danger to myself or others; nevertheless, the doors and windows were bolted, and there seemed no chance of getting out that night. In any case, I knew I needed to be hospitalized: going back home and into the care of my poor overwhelmed husband was not an option. So, for half an hour I did nothing but pace up and down, up and down, in front of the glass-fronted nurses' station, occasionally stopping to knock on the glass and ask when my things (my allowable things, that is) would be returned to me. I wanted, in particular, my stuffed elephant. "Soon," they said kindly but firmly. "We're just in the middle of a shift change. Soon."

There were five or six other inmates, men and women, sitting or milling about in the large dayroom. One or two said hello; I ignored them. *Pretty Woman* was showing on the big television that hung on one wall, the volume cranked up loud. After a while I broke out of my up-and-down pattern and began to explore the room. On a long shelf under the window were jigsaw puzzles, games, and art supplies; I opened one puzzle box, emptied out a few of the one thousand pieces, and abandoned that idea immediately. I went and studied the bookcase, which held a vast assortment of ancient

---

* The approved term these days is *behavioral health ward*, but I eschew that term because neither I nor most of the other patients there were hospitalized for misbehaving.

magazines and a somewhat smaller assortment of used books. One of them was *Fierce Conversations* by Susan Scott. I knew that book! I had actually referenced it in one of my own books, published four years earlier. I picked it up, clutched it to my chest, and continued pacing: up and down, round and round, ignoring everyone and everything, trying to breathe, telling myself I would be all right, all right, all right.

Finally, at about eight p.m., a nurse approached and asked if we could talk for a bit. She introduced herself as Wendy as she ushered me over to a small table that sat just outside the nurses' station. Blonde and sweet-faced, she couldn't have been more than 26 or 27. We sat down, and she proceeded to do the intake interview, which is when they ask you lots of questions about your situation: mental, physical, emotional, and social. I don't remember thinking anything about her except that she seemed nice. I had been taking Ambien Controlled Release, 12.5 milligrams, for sleep; Wendy said, with apparently real regret, that the hospital didn't have the controlled-release version but that they could give me the regular type, 5 milligrams.

"Fine," I said, too exhausted to argue about anything anymore. "But I'm warning you, I'll be up at one thirty."

"OK," said Wendy. "And when that happens, we have options. We can give you some Ativan, for example. Don't worry. I'm right here, all night, and I'm going to look after you."

I did indeed wake up at one thirty, and Wendy did indeed offer me some Ativan, which I took, again too tired to object to any meds they cared to throw at me. I went back to bed, awoke at I didn't know what time, stumbled out into the dayroom, looked at the clock, saw it was six thirty, and nearly fell over in shock. I hadn't slept that long or soundly in months. Wendy was standing right there. "You slept all the way through!" she said, obviously delighted for me.

As the days crept by—filled with doctor visits, group therapy, medication times, meals, snacks, "recreation," television, more meals and snacks, and, hallelujah, *napping*, which I'd been unable to do for ages—Wendy became my favorite nurse. She worked the night shift, Wednesday to Sunday. I missed her during the daytimes. During my two-week stay I identified two types of nurses, whom I dubbed the pros and the saints. The pros were perfectly competent and courteous but a bit hardened, going about things with a no-nonsense air, for which I could hardly blame them; that's how I'd behave if I had their grueling job. But the saints, of which there were only a few, clearly had a calling: their empathy was genuine, their patience inexhaustible, their demeanor consistently cheerful. Wendy was the saintliest of the saints: the bodhisattva of the psych ward.

Here are a few of the things that made her stand out: Unlike most of the other nurses, who would call me over to the table when it was time to take my vitals, Nurse Wendy would roll the cart to wherever I was sitting. Rather than just sticking the thermometer in my mouth, she would ask permission to take my temperature. If I asked her for a fill-up of my water cup, she remembered I liked it without ice. Instead of deciding when it was time for my evening medications, she'd ask me what time I wanted to take them. She let me use my phone, unsupervised, for longer than the prescribed ten minutes a day.

But most important, Wendy talked with me. At night, I would often be in bed when she brought me my meds; at first I was too sick and afraid to say much, but as time passed, I began to open up a little. She kept things professional, but she was more willing than the other nurses to spend time chatting. When I asked her opinion on my condition, she said I was definitely getting better. "Think about when you first came in," she said. "You were beside yourself. Look at you now: you're able to focus on a book!" Truth be told, I couldn't *really* focus on a book—I'd been reading the same three pages of a mystery novel for as many days—but hearing Wendy say it made me think maybe I could. I told her what the chief doctor had said that day in our conference; she said Doctor D. was great, that the ward had a great team who all supported one another. I asked her if there was hope for me; she assured me there was hope, and more than hope. Her face radiated kindness, sympathy, pleasure.

On the last night she was on duty before I was to be discharged, I thanked her for everything. Standing by my bed, she clasped her hands at her waist and said, with a serene smile and just a touch of emotion: "It has been my honor and privilege to care for you, Jocelyn."

Learning from the Empath

The Empath is the only one of the archetypes who receives full approval from the patriarchy.* Women are supposed to be empaths: kind and understanding, able to sort out problems using our "woman's intuition," ever quick with a consoling word and a sympathetic nod. Angels of Mercy, as they say. And indeed, there is plenty of evidence, both scientific and humanistic, that women, on average, tune into emotions and listen better than men do. If we lean on these strengths, are we falling into the trap of male expectations and stereotypes?

I say we shouldn't worry about what's approved and what isn't. Breaking stereotypes just for the sake of it is a false triumph; moreover, as the Miaoshan story suggests, real compassion has a cool, steely, powerful core. To draw on the power of the Empath, we can:

Listen and confirm. It's a fact that most of us, when we're supposed to be listening, are actually planning what we're going to say next—maybe because we think we're obliged, when faced with someone in distress, to offer something useful. I've been struck, however, by how useful it's been to me when I was in distress to have someone simply, truly listen. Nurse Wendy was an excellent listener, and there have been others: friends, colleagues, even random acquaintances I happened to encounter in a moment of need. How do we show someone we're truly listening? By staying silent for as long as necessary, then confirming what we've heard—which is not the same as agreeing. It's especially important to confirm the emotions the person has expressed: "That sounds scary." "You're angry because of what Jane said." "How frustrating!" "I know this has been difficult for you." "I'm so sorry; I can tell you loved her."

The sales and service training programs offered by my old company taught this principle: "Attend to feelings first, facts second." If an upset customer

---

* One might count the Amiga as another one, but she, if recognized for her ally-making skills, is too often deemed manipulative. And Savitri, the Death-befriending Amiga we met in chapter 5, is turned by today's (male) storytellers into an example of wifely devotion, her negotiating chops completely overlooked.

doesn't believe his or her feelings have been heard and understood, all your fact-based solutions, no matter how well-considered, will sound like the grownups in a Peanuts cartoon: *Wah-wah-waaaaaaah.* Conversely, think about the times (perhaps few) when you were suffering and someone really listened and acknowledged your pain. Think about the difference it made to you. That is Empath magic.

Err toward generosity. A former boss of mine made this his maxim. The generosity he was talking about didn't have to do with money or perks; it had to do with ascribing to others good intent and treating them accordingly. Miaoshan/Guanyin is an extreme, mythic example of such generosity, but to me, her donation of eyes and hands is not the most extraordinary part of the story; more extraordinary is the reason she gives: "to repay the king's love." I don't think she means it sarcastically. As a bodhisattva, she's able to see beyond her father's appalling badness to the goodness he might exhibit in the future and that perhaps was there all along: a love that lay buried beneath layers of rage and narcissism until it was unearthed by her grace.

Of course, we non-bodhisattvas are not called upon to make such drastic leaps of faith toward people who have injured us. But we can, I think, be like Nurse Wendy, who rolled the vitals cart over to me and let me use my phone unsupervised. Such acts of generosity require judgment; had I been the sort to call my drug dealer, Wendy would have been unwise to leave me alone. She knew I was not that sort, and wisely gave me what autonomy she could. Her last words to me—that it had been *her* honor and privilege to care for *me*, the psych patient—are an example of the Empath's magnanimity, which is found in small gestures as much as big ones.

Be an objective eye. I mentioned how strange I found it at first that Miaoshan would spend much of her time "admonishing." I came to understand her sternness as a byproduct of her caring: caring enough to try to show others a way out of their suffering. A person in mental distress often can't get far enough out of their head, so to speak, in order to see how their own habits and thought patterns are contributing to their misfortune. A real bodhisattva, a real Empath, offers the needed outside perspective–the tough love, if you will–without fear of conflict or of being disliked.

But it can work the other way, too: an Empath can often see the positive things the suffering one can't. When Nurse Wendy said, "Look at you, able to focus on a book!" I realized that even though I'd been reading the same three pages over and over, I was at least reading–something that had been impossible only a week before. I hadn't seen the change. Wendy had, and her seeing it made me believe I was getting better. One of the strongest ways we can influence others is by pointing out their strengths: what they're good at, what they're doing well. These qualities, apparent to us, are rarely as apparent to the one who possesses them. When we "admonish" that person to recognize them, we're giving a gift only an Empath can give.

8

THE ESCAPIST

PENELOPE'S HUSBAND, ODYSSEUS, SAILED OFF to the war in Troy almost twenty years ago and has not yet returned. For the past four years Penelope, queen of Ithaca, has been persecuted by a gang of rude and rowdy suitors who trash her house, eat her livestock, and drink her wine. They refuse to leave until she chooses one of them to marry. *Odysseus is dead*, they say. She must pick a new spouse, or they'll keep hanging around. The ancient rules of hospitality protect them as guests and forbid her from throwing them out.

But Penelope is the equal in wiles of her famously wily husband, and she devises a plan to delay. "I will choose someone," she says, "after I've finished weaving this funeral cloth for my father-in-law, Laertes; how shameful if he died and I hadn't provided him with a shroud appropriate to his rank!" The men agree to wait until she completes the project.

Three and a half years later, her grown son, Telemachus, is railing at Antinous, de facto leader of the suitors, for consuming his inheritance. *Not our fault*, says Antinous. *We know what your mother's been doing*:

By day she'd weave at her great and growing web—
By night, by the light of torches set beside her,
She would unravel all she'd done. Three whole years
She deceived us blind, seduced us with this scheme...[1]

But now, Antinous says, they're onto her. She won't escape this time.

Penelope: Artful Dodger

As with Savitri (see chapter 5), many modern commentators have focused on Penelope's devotion and fidelity to her husband; after all, she stays true to Odysseus over twenty long years, not knowing whether he's alive or dead but suspecting the latter due to the dangers of sea voyages and a lack of reliable reports—all the while rejecting multiple marriage offers. I maintain, however, that the most interesting aspect of this Grecian queen's character is not her devotion, but her dodginess: she is the Escapist.

The Escapist is **wily**. Tricks are her métier. Odysseus was famous for his trickiness, and indeed has been called womanish for it, classical scholars tending to reserve their greatest admiration for manly, straight-on fighters such as Achilles and Hector. But wiliness, it must be admitted, often wins the day. Odysseus was the one who devised a giant hollow wooden horse (the Trojan Horse of myth) as a way to get the Greek army inside the enemy's walls, resulting in Troy's defeat. Then there was the incident with Polyphemus the Cyclops, who trapped Odysseus and his crew on an island, intending to eat them. Odysseus introduced himself to the fearsome monster as "Nobody," so that after he had jabbed out its one eye with a burning wood stake, blinding it, and the other Cyclopes had arrived shouting out, "What's wrong?"—Polyphemus roared, "*Nobody* has blinded me! *Nobody* is to blame!" The others retreated, shrugging, and Odysseus and his men managed to flee.

But clever as those tricks were, they were short-lived, whereas Penelope's ruse must be sustained for the long term if she is to avoid remarriage. She contrives the "can't marry anyone until I finish my father-in-law's shroud" excuse and keeps it up for more than three years, weaving the cloth by day and picking it apart by night. No doubt the suitors' constant drunkenness and fornication with the maidservants make the con easier; still, it's an impressive run of guile. "A fine mind and subtle wiles too," says Antinous. "No one could equal Penelope for intrigue."[2]

The Escapist is also **nonconfrontational**. Not for her the battles of the Amazon or Claimant: when there's trouble, she avoids it. And unlike the Amiga and Mesmerist, she doesn't even try to influence her adversaries: she simply waits, evades, and lies low. Of all the archetypes, she is best at the fine art of leaning *out*. When a tearful Penelope instructs a bard to cease his sad song of warriors journeying home from Troy, her son Telemachus chastises her, telling her to return to her quarters and let the men give the orders. She withdraws without a word (though continues weeping in her chamber). Nor does she berate the suitors to their face; she knows if she engages in direct conflict with them, she will lose.

A maid eventually tattles, and the weaving-unweaving plot is discovered. Antinous tells Penelope to drop the charade and get on with it. She knows she has to choose: Odysseus himself told her before he left that once she saw the beard on their son's cheek, she should pick a new husband. Thanks to the greedy house party, her wealth is diminishing by the day. Her parents are pressuring her to remarry. And, while Telemachus wishes he were man enough to eject the villains on his own, he knows he isn't. Penelope is growing desperate.

It is at this point that a wandering beggar arrives at the estate, asking for food and shelter. He's a past-middle-aged, wretchedly dressed but powerfully built man who claims to have been in the war and moreover to have seen, quite recently with his own eyes, Odysseus–alive. Of course this "beggar" is Odysseus himself, in disguise. He reveals his identity only to Telemachus, who falls on his father's neck exclaiming for joy, but Odysseus tells him not to spill the secret yet; they must first plan how to deal with the suitors, which won't be easy. So Telemachus invites the "beggar" in, gives him bread, and gives him leave to make the rounds of the guests in order to beg alms from them, too. All oblige except Antinous, who hurls insults, then a stool, striking the ragged man square in the back.

"Cautious Queen Penelope," in her chamber, hears of Antinous's brutality. She shows traits of the Empath, saying to her faithful old servingwoman:

> They're all hateful,
> plotting their vicious plots. But Antinous
> is the worst of all—he's black death itself.
> Here's this luckless stranger, wandering down
> the halls and begging scraps—hard-pressed by need—
> and the rest all give the man his fill of food
> but that one gives him a footstool
> hurled at his right shoulder, hits his back![3]

She calls in the swineherd Eumaeus, one of the few servants still loyal to Odysseus, and tells him to bring the stranger to her. "I'd like to give him a warm welcome," she says, "ask [him] if he's heard some news about my gallant husband or seen him in the flesh."[4] Eumaeus, greatly excited, goes to deliver the message—but Odysseus says he fears the mob's further abuse, so please to tell the queen he'll come to the hall that night, when things have calmed down. Then she may ask him all the questions she likes.

Out on the porch additional brawls ensue, in which Odysseus impresses the rowdies with his strength and fighting skill. But at length twilight descends, and Penelope appears in the hall beautifully coiffed and dressed, drawing gasps of admiration from the men. We are told that the goddess Athena has inspired her to display herself thus "to fan their hearts"; we wonder, however, whether she already has an intuition about the stranger's true identity. When one of the men steps forward to praise her, she demurs: "Any beauty I once had was destroyed when Odysseus sailed away," she says, and goes on to make a lengthy speech (which the disguised Odysseus hears) about her fidelity to her husband, the torment she has experienced, and (most cleverly) the mortification she feels due to her supposed suitors eating *her* food rather than following custom and bringing their own calves and lambs in a bid to win her favor. Odysseus, we are told, "glow[s] with joy to hear all this—his wife's trickery luring gifts from her suitors now ... but all the while with something else in mind."[5]

Penelope's speech buys her a little more time, because each suitor immediately sends a lackey to go get a gift. The to-ing and fro-ing, presentations, and drinking that ensue give Odysseus and Telemachus a chance to stow the suitors' weapons out of reach. At last, with the men in a stupor and Telemachus gone to bed, Penelope and the "stranger" are left alone by the fire, where they have a long chat about Odysseus, whom the "stranger" claims to have seen alive and well. Penelope confesses she is out of ideas for delay and says that on the morrow she will stage a contest: the man who is able to string Odysseus's great bow and shoot an arrow straight through the holes in twelve ax-heads set in a row in the great hall—he is the man she will marry. Odysseus urges her on: "Before that crew can handle the polished bow ... Odysseus, man of exploits, will be home with you!"[6]

The next day, Penelope announces the contest. The stranger says he too will participate, raising howls of outrage from the men: "Not a shred of sense in your head, filthy drifter!" cries Antinous. But Penelope—in what may be her only open show of opposition—says the poor man should be allowed to compete, for on the off chance he wins, he surely won't have the gall to insist on marrying her. "If he succeeds," she says, "I'll give him a new set of clothes and a sword." So the competition proceeds, with each suitor trying and failing in turn. Most cannot even manage to string the incredibly stiff bow; the stranger, however, remains seated as he strings the bow with ease and fires an arrow clean through the twelve axes. And once he does, the fight is on: he strips off his rags, leaps atop a table, calls Telemachus to his side, and father and son embark on a bloodbath for the ages. The suitors, surprised without their weapons to hand, are sitting ducks. Antinous is the first to fall. In a short time, all are dead.

Ever since Penelope made her speech to the hall, we've been growing more and more certain she knows who the stranger really is. Why else would she arrange such a contest and insist he be allowed to enter? Now, with her persecutors dead and Odysseus having revealed himself, surely she'll fly to his arms.

But the wily Escapist is also wary. **Slow to trust**, she hesitates to commit herself.

During the slaughter, the goddess Athena has kept Penelope in a magical sleep. Now the queen is awakened by her servingwoman, who relays the joyful news: *It is he, Odysseus! He has come home and killed the brutes!* "The gods have made you mad," says Penelope. "Or else, if what you say is true, it must be a god in disguise." She goes downstairs and upon seeing Odysseus, hangs back, suspicious. Telemachus pitches a small fit: What sort of cold greeting is this for his father? But now it's Penelope's turn to chastise: "If he is truly Odysseus," she says, "make no mistake: we two will know each other . . . we two have secret signs, known to us both, but hidden from the world."[7] (We hear her implication: *And hidden from you, too, sonny.*)

Odysseus laughs and tells Telemachus to drop the matter; later, however, when it's time for bed and Penelope is still doubtful, he too grows offended. "Strange woman! . . . What other wife could have a spirit so unbending?" He announces that he'll sleep alone, for "she has a heart of iron in her breast."[8] But Penelope has one more trick up her sleeve. She instructs her maidservants to move the bedstead out of her chamber so the stranger can sleep in it. Odysseus angrily points out that this will be impossible, for he built the chamber and bed with his own hands, using the trunk of a live, rooted olive tree to make the bedpost. "There's our secret sign, I tell you, our life story! Does our bed, my lady, still stand planted firm? . . . Or has someone chopped away the olive trunk and hauled our bedstead off?"[9]

At last Penelope knows he's the real thing. Wary no more, she goes to him and covers his face with kisses: "So joyous now to her the sight of her husband, vivid in her gaze."[10]

Pam: Keeping Her Head Down

Conventional wisdom says the only way to deal with bullies is to stand up to them. Today's workplace gurus would advise Penelope to tell those suitors in no uncertain terms that she'll not tolerate their behavior and, if they persist, to report them to HR. The Escapist, however, knows something many of us don't: When it comes to harassers and abusers, whether of the physical or emotional type, you can't "make them stop." Only *you* can stop; that is, stop engaging with them.

"Disengage" is the best advice I didn't take. Back in 2012, my company was dealing with a new president ("Bruce" of chapter 3) and his irritable boss, our CEO, who for reasons too tedious to explain had, unbeknownst to us employees, embarked on a secret campaign of reading our email in order to identify supposed troublemakers. He was within his rights to do so, for there was a line in the employee handbook stating that one's work emails belonged to the firm and were not to be considered private. In any case, the tea leaves had been clear to read for several months: Bruce and the CEO were in cost-cutting mode, and they considered my R&D team a cost center, ripe for elimination. No longer were we among the most respected, secure groups in the firm. Seeing storm clouds looming and angered by our treatment, I began laying plans to leave. I rang up a former colleague who had started his own successful training company and asked his advice. Here's what he said:

"Now that you've made the decision to go, you'll be tempted to say 'screw it.' You'll want to tell people off. *Don't.* Keep quiet, focus on finding the next thing, and walk out with dignity."

I thanked him and assured him I would do just that.

Then I did nothing of the sort. Instead I lunged for the opposite side of the archetypes wheel and loosed my inner Amazon, minus the noble intent of a real Amazon. I thought I was fighting for my team, but really I was just kicking up a fuss. I also fell into the Medusa Trap, letting my scorn for my bosses show on my face and also (very stupidly) in a few emails, which the CEO found and read. A few of my team members did the same, sending their own jokey missives, which were also discovered. The results: I handed in my letter of resignation and was told they'd been planning to fire me anyway; one of my team members was sacked for "misconduct"; another was verbally shredded by the CEO and quit a few weeks after that; and several other people were redeployed into less-desirable jobs. By the time the dust had settled, the R&D team's size had been reduced by 75 percent, the budget slashed to a pittance, and everyone was in a rage, a panic, or both.

Except for Pam.

Pam was a vice president in R&D whose job was to develop our online learning methods. She had been with the firm even longer than I had—almost 24 years—playing various roles from customer service rep to salesperson to project manager to consultant. She was smart, versatile, and a quick study. She was also conflict-averse: although she held her own in discussions, I can't think of a single time she got in a fight with anyone. Her demeanor was always pleasant, always positive. If a misunderstanding arose, she was quick to apologize.

I came to learn, though, that she had plenty of opinions, some of them non-innocuous. A few years prior I'd asked if I could use her virtual classroom account for a meeting I was leading. "Sure," she said, and gave me her password. When I logged in, I noticed that the chat window was full of text; Pam had apparently forgotten to clear it after her last use of the software. There in the window I saw a private discussion between her and a work friend in which they were venting their frustration with one of my other team members. My eyebrows went up as I glanced through it. The comments were blunt—though, I had to admit, fair. Unlike our CEO, I'd been taught it was wrong to read other people's private correspondence, so after a few moments of fascinated scrolling I closed the chat and left it closed as I went on with my meeting. But afterward, I reflected on how Pam had a stronger point of view than appearances would suggest. If anything, this increased my respect for her, because I realized her nonconfrontational style was a choice: a choice based not in wimpiness but in prudence.

When the crap hit the fan and the rest of us were busy being fired, screamed at, or demoted, Pam kept her head down. She had not participated in the email kibitzing, so the two bosses had nothing on her. They acknowledged as much when, shortly after my departure, they contacted her to "check in."

"We know you weren't involved in any of the misconduct," they said.

"What misconduct?" she asked.

A week or two later, she gave me a call. I asked how she was doing. "Fine," she said, "but I'm getting out. It's not safe here anymore. And I can see there's no point waiting around to be laid off, because there aren't going to be any severance payments." I said that was probably true. She then apologized to me for not protesting her teammates' treatment. "I can't afford to lose my job," she said. "So I've decided for the time being, I'm just going to tell management what they want to hear. I'm going to be Get-Along Girl." I said I thought that was smart. What purpose would it serve for her to stir the pot further? What good would it do for her to wade into a fight she couldn't win?

Within a year, the self-proclaimed Get-Along Girl had landed a new and better job at another company. You might assume she'd stay far away forever, but no: a year after that, she returned to the old firm. "I hadn't burned any bridges," she told me later, "so when things became more favorable, I was able to come back—at a much higher salary." And when the place again failed to suit her, she moved on. In each case, she (unlike me) followed the sage advice of my former colleague: *Keep quiet, focus on finding the next thing, and walk out with dignity.*

Here's how Pam explained her powers of elusion:

> I sometimes bashed my bosses, but I *never* put it in writing. My mother had worked on top-secret government projects, so I was schooled in the dangers of documentation; this made my escape easier, since I left no evidence. Also, I avoided interaction with anyone I felt was disingenuous or slimy. I ran into one of those managers later, at another organization, and I avoided him like the plague though he tried to engage with me. Again, I had training from a young age that you don't have to agree with everyone, and when you don't, saying nothing is often the best strategy.

Learning from the Escapist

Celebrities must cope with stalkers, harassers, even kidnappers and murderers. When they need help, they turn to Gavin de Becker, a world-renowned security consultant. One of the best resources I've found for a would-be Escapist—and for women in general—is de Becker's book *The Gift of Fear*.[11] Many of the ideas below are his.

Disengage. As I said a few pages back, you can't make a bully stop. You can only stop *yourself*; that is, stop engaging with him.*

"What about the Amazon?" you ask. "Doesn't she fight bullies?" Yes, she does. But the true Amazon (see chapter 2) fights for a cause and persuades others to join her. If you're faced with a hostile work environment created by one or more bullies *and* you can get others on board with your fight for justice, playing the Amazon can work; if, however, you have been singled out for abuse and others see it as not-their-problem, your best bet is not to go to war, but to disengage. That means doing whatever it takes to exit the relationship. "I'm not in a relationship with him," you say, but you're wrong: as long as you're "trying to make him stop" you are indeed in a relationship—one that consists of him bullying you and you trying to make him stop. Any interaction with such a person only buys you more of the same treatment. If you go for two weeks without responding and then give in and shoot him a text, he simply learns that two weeks is the price he must pay to get a response out of you. The wisest course is not to interact at all. As de Becker says: "Best response? No response."

Or, as my mother used to say: "If the boys tease you, ignore them." Nowadays, that advice is considered regressive. We're supposed to teach our daughters to stand up for themselves, to *do* something about bullying. But ignoring a bully *is* doing something. It takes strength of character to get fifteen baiting text messages from someone and never reply, just as it takes strength of character to walk away from an abusive boyfriend. The

---

* In this section I will use "him" to refer to a bully, since the worst abusers of women tend to be men. That's not to say women can't be bullies; I've run across quite a few bullies of the female sort, and the same advice applies to dealing with them.

Escapist is no coward. She knows what she wants, and what she wants is to have nothing to do with that guy.

Total disengagement is not always possible. Maybe the bully is your boss, and you can't find another job right now. But even in such cases, the thing to do (usually) is to disengage as much as you can.* Maintain a calm, professional demeanor. Rise to no bait. Join in no banter. Set boundaries. And speaking of boundaries . . .

Learn to say "No." Penelope says no to her suitors and goes on saying it for three and half years. Many women, unfortunately, have never been taught to say no and therefore find it difficult to say the word even once. We can also find it hard to say *only* no; we feel we must elaborate on our reasons, offer excuses, let him down easy. "It's me, not you," we explain with an apologetic tilt of the head. "You see, I just need some space right now. I'm having some family issues. Plus, I'm so busy at work. Maybe some other time."

"No" is a complete sentence, notes de Becker. He offers this script for those of us who need to deal with a pursuer who hasn't listened to our repeated, polite requests to get lost:

> No matter what you may have assumed till now, and no matter for what reason you assumed it, I have no romantic interest in you whatsoever. I am certain I never will. I expect that knowing this, you'll put your attention elsewhere, which I understand, because that's what I intend to do.[12] [End of statement.]

Such an explicit rejection may sound harsh, but it's necessary if hints haven't worked. And this strategy applies not only to overeager swains, but to unwanted chasers and pests of all kinds in our business and personal lives. After such a "no," your next step is to disengage completely. If the

---

* Of course if his behavior constitutes sexual harassment or is otherwise illegal, that's a different story. Then you should document everything and report him to the appropriate authorities. But even then, maintaining physical and emotional distance is always a wise choice.

stalker persists, says de Becker, your resolve should be strengthened, not challenged. You have set the boundary; now you maintain it, for as long as it takes.

Embrace the gift of fear. When Pam called me after my departure, one of the first things she said was, "It's not safe here anymore." I was struck by that, because she (I thought) had no reason to worry about losing her job or retribution from management; after all, she had kept her head down during the mayhem and, in the bosses' eyes, was a well-behaved employee. But she was right: it wasn't safe. There were further shake-ups to come, and more important, the place had shifted from a culture of benevolence and trust to one of animosity and suspicion. Pam had a gut sense that the wolves were on the prowl. She would not stick around to be eaten.

Fear, says de Becker, is a gift. The small but urgent voice rising from our subconscious, telling us something's wrong—"it's not safe here"—is a powerful protective device. The Escapist, better than any other archetype, makes use of it.

The next time you hear that voice, don't dismiss it. Don't tell yourself, "I'm just being silly, everything's fine."

You're not being silly. Get out.

9

THE SNOW QUEEN

"WHO DARES TO MOCK ME?" [1]

Isolde, princess of Ireland, is being transported by ship to Cornwall, where she is to marry King Marke. Escorting her is Tristan, the king's loyal retainer and (as we shall later learn) an old acquaintance of hers. As the ship skims eastward over the waves we hear wafting from high on the masthead the song of a young sailor: "Fresh the wind blows towards home; my Irish child, where are you now?... Irish girl, you wild, adorable girl!"

Isolde assumes the words are a sneer at her. Indignant, she demands of her maidservant, Brangäne, "Who dares?" then proceeds to vent her ire at the "insolent ship," wishing it wrecked by storm winds. Brangäne, much distressed, begs Isolde to say what ails her: Why did she leave her parents with barely a parting word? Why on the voyage has she stayed "mute, pale and silent," neither eating nor sleeping?

Isolde does not reply. Instead she gestures to the curtain of the tented cabin, crying out, "Air! Air! My heart is stifled. Open up! Open wide there!"

Brangäne throws open the curtain, revealing Tristan at the ship's helm. Isolde stands, her golden hair blowing in the salt breeze, regarding him with a keen, cold eye.

Isolde: Mistress of Silence

The Snow Queen resides at the far north of the archetypes wheel. A creature of the frosty air, she is, as my work friend once half-jokingly called me, uptight and unfriendly. Yet Isolde is also a famous lover—she and Tristan are among the most famous lovers in all Western literature, second only to Romeo and Juliet—so you might wonder why I've chosen her to represent a type that is anything but warm.

In *The Romance of Tristan and Iseult*, M. Joseph Bedier's self-proclaimed definitive version of a legend that was told in myriad forms all over medieval Europe, Iseult is a fairly flat, insipid character; the story focuses on Tristan's torrid emotions and daring exploits. But in Richard Wagner's 1865 opera, Isolde (as she is called in German) is the star.* She gets the first and last words, the main musical themes, and the renowned "Love-Death" (*liebestod*) song at the end, the music of which is often used in films and television shows featuring doomed amour. Moreover, her character here is much more complex than in the *Romance*: her feelings for Tristan cannot be attributed merely to the love potion that, traditionally, is the cause of their attraction, and even after she consumes the potion, there is something about her desire that is, how shall we say? Chaste? Dreamlike? Removed? In any case, no come-hither Temptress is she.

Isolde's opening line, "Who dares to mock me?" points to the Snow Queen's **disdainful pride**. Isolde's disdain vibrates through most of act 1, first as she tells Brangäne to go demand that Tristan attend her—"Let my

---

* Supposedly the favorite composer of Hitler, Wagner is a figure some nowadays find distasteful. To repeat, I do not hold up any of these writers and artists as a personal role model, and I am not interested in their private or political views. I am interested in their works, most especially the female characters they created.

command teach the vainglorious one to fear his mistress, Isolde!"[2]—and then, when he will not come, as she relates the story of their meeting. We learn that some months ago, she found an unconscious wounded man floating in a small boat along the shoreline near her home. She rescued him and nursed him back to health. He called himself "Tantris." When she noticed his notched sword and fitted the notch to the shard that had been left in the severed head of Morold, her betrothed, who had gone to collect tribute from Cornwall, she realized that "Tantris" was in fact Tristan, Morold's killer. But as she raised the sword to strike him dead in vengeance, Tristan looked into her eyes, and (she says) his wretchedness stayed her hand. She dropped the sword. (Remember, the Snow Queen is only two steps away from the Empath and many steps away from the Amazon.)

Once healed, Tristan returned to Cornwall, told King Marke of the fair-haired Irish princess, and offered to negotiate a marriage. Now Isolde is being shipped to her new husband like a chattel. Perceiving herself betrayed by the man she helped, she is in high dudgeon:

> If Morold were alive, who would have ever dared to bring such shame upon us? For this vassal, prince of the Cornish, to suit for the crown of Ireland! Ah, I am lost… The avenging sword, instead of wielding it, I impotently let it fall! Now I am in the vassal's bondage![3]

The Snow Queen is also **silently aloof**. The most introverted of the archetypes, she keeps to herself and keeps her counsel. Isolde does not reveal the true identity of "Tantris" until she has almost arrived in Cornwall, and then only to Brangäne. "She who in silence gave him his life, from the enemy's fury quietly hid him," she says, and "silently lent her sanctuary to save him…"[4] As she speaks on, we begin to see she loves Tristan and hates the thought of being married to another while being near him every day; she will not express her feelings directly, however, and Brangäne assumes Isolde is merely worried that King Marke, her husband-to-be, will not love her. Brangäne assures her mistress there is an answer to that problem: a love potion brewed by Isolde's mother, a renowned sorceress. Isolde perks up then, rummaging in the chest, but it's not the love potion she seeks—rather, a flask of deadly poison.

At this point Tristan's retainer shows up to tell the ladies to prepare, for they are about to make land. Isolde, haughty as ever, insists she will not walk with Tristan to meet the king unless he, Tristan, first comes to seek her forgiveness for "unatoned guilt." While the retainer is delivering the message, Isolde tells Brangäne to prepare the death draught. Brangäne falls back, horrified and confused, as Isolde composes herself for Tristan's arrival.

He comes and stands respectfully at the entrance. "Demand, my lady, what you wish," he says. Isolde asks why he ignored her before, to which he replies, "Respect held me in awe."

Isolde is having none of it. "You showed me little enough respect; with blatant mockery you refused to obey my command." After more back-and-forth, she finally spits it out: "A debt of blood exists between us!"[5] She reminds Tristan what she did for him when he was in her power: "When in my quiet chamber [you] lay sick, and I stood quietly before [you] with the sword, my lips were silent, I held my hand."[6] Now, she says, she will discharge her oath to take revenge for Morold's murder (and, we suspect, for Tristan's rejection). Tristan offers her his sword, which she refuses; instead, she says, "let us drink reconciliation." She motions to Brangäne to bring the cup, but Tristan seems lost in thought. "What have you to say to me?" demands Isolde.

"The mistress of silence bids me say nothing," he replies.[7]

At last Isolde persuades him to drink. Tristan clearly knows what's coming and welcomes it: "Beneficent draught of forgetfulness," he says, "I drain you unwaveringly."[8]

He lifts the cup and drinks, but Isolde snatches it back with, "Half is mine! Traitor! I drink to you!" She downs the rest and throws the goblet aside.

Of course Brangäne, desperate, has substituted love potion for poison. Minutes pass as Isolde and Tristan first gaze at each other in defiance, then are seized with tremors, look down in confusion, and finally look up again— not with defiance now, but with all-consuming desire:

Isolde (her voice trembling): Tristan!

Tristan (overcome): Isolde!

Isolde (sinking on his breast): Faithless darling!

Tristan (ardently embracing her): Blessed lady!

Pretty hot stuff. And yet not so, for from that moment the two lovers do everything except consummate their union. In act 2, they meet secretly at night in a castle garden; sing of their love, the bondage of life, and the freedom of death; sing some more as they recline close together on a grassy bank; and are eventually discovered by King Marke and his henchmen. In act 3, Tristan, wounded in the fight, flees to his childhood home and there—musing still about love and life, freedom and death—awaits Isolde. When she finally arrives, he tears off his bandage, opening up his wound as he runs to embrace her. He expires in her arms.

King Marke shows up again. Everything has been explained to him by Brangäne, and he is now ready to forgive the couple, allowing them to marry, but it is too late. Isolde pays him no mind. She sings the *liebestod*, in which she describes her vision of Tristan alive and glowing, and finally sinks down on his body to lie inert. Is she dead, or is she somehow transformed? Each interpretation has its proponents. One thing is clear: sex is not what these two lovers have ever had in mind.

I don't mean to sound dismissive (although as a wintery type myself, dismissiveness is my specialty); Wagner's music is beyond compare, and his lyrics are nothing to sneeze at, either. My point is simply that Isolde's passion does nothing to change or diminish her status as Snow Queen, for that passion is all air and water, no earth or fire. With her love, she seeks to **transcend the world**. Here is what she sings as she stands gazing at the dead Tristan in the final scene, aware of nothing and no one around her:

Friends! Look! Do you not feel and see it? Do I alone hear this melody so wondrously and gently sounding from within him ...soaring aloft, its sweet echoes resounding about me? Are they gentle aerial waves ringing out clearly, surging around me? Are they billows of blissful fragrance? . . . Shall I breathe, shall I give ear! Shall I drink of them, plunge beneath them? Breathe my life away in sweet scents? In the heaving swell, in the resounding echoes, in the universal stream of the world-breath . . .[9]

Billows and waves. We're reminded of her cry in act 1: "Air! Air! My heart is stifled!"

Throughout acts 2 and 3, both Isolde and Tristan equate bright day with prison, dark night with freedom. Love, as they experience it, is a thing of mist and shadows. The forever-night of death will, they believe, allow them to escape the bondage of the sunlit world with its harsh scrutiny and weighty conventions. They will turn their face away from the garish light of day (to borrow a line from *The Phantom of the Opera*), and at last they will be together, free.

But while Tristan's longing for death is straightforward—he rips off his bandage in order to kill himself and succeeds in that purpose—the same does not seem true of Isolde. Unlike Shakespeare's Juliet, she drinks no poison, plunges no knife. In the end she merely sinks gently into Brangäne's arms and then down onto Tristan's body, singing: "To drown, to founder—unconscious—utmost rapture!" The stage directions indicate that King Marke "blesses the bodies." But what exactly has happened to Isolde is unclear.

I think she is not dead, but transfigured. For one thing, although she is angry with Tristan when she finds he did not wait for her so they could spend a final hour together ("Spiteful man! Will you punish me thus with this most harsh of sentences?"), she shows not the slightest sadness during the *liebestod*. She is all ecstasy, "soaring aloft." As well, the Isolde we came to know in act 1 is just fine with solitary life, and in the opera's closing moments we sense she is more than fine with her glorious, solitary vision: a vision that includes her lover, to be sure, but in which her lover is almost incidental. As Tristan recedes into the wondrous music, soft aerial waves, and billows of sweet fragrance, Isolde is left in her bliss, joined not to Tristan but to the universal stream of the world-breath.

"Do I alone hear this melody?" she wonders aloud. We suspect yes. The Snow Queen, whom the cold never bothered anyway, dwells in northern aeries: rapturous, silent, apart.

Isabel: She's So Cold

Isabel was in my year at Swarthmore, a liberal-arts college outside Philadelphia. Though flat chested and socially awkward, she was dubbed by some "the prettiest girl in the freshman class." Her tall blondeness was complemented by an air of aloofness, which, her mother had once told her, made her appealing to the boys.

And so she was. From the week she arrived until graduation day, she was never without a boyfriend plus one or two suitors waiting in the wings. Her friends were often annoyed with her, not because she attracted and slept with a lot of men (it was the early 1980s, so nothing unusual in that) but because she took it all so seriously, proclaiming herself madly in love and then, when the next chap came along, proclaiming mad love for him—or terrible indecision about whom to choose. Drama swirled around Isabel, but she herself seemed relatively untouched by it all, talking little about her affairs of the heart and maintaining a stoic demeanor as the romantic storms raged. Unlike many women, her inclination during a messy breakup was not to run to her girlfriends for wine and sympathy in late-night tell-all sessions; instead she would withdraw into her shell, spending most of her time with the new guy, doubling down on her studies, and ignoring everything and everyone else. She was easy to get along with—so attested her roommate—but hard to get to know. She kept most people at arm's length. One young woman who had lost a beau to Isabel denounced her as a "dull cookie."

In the second semester of her freshman year, Isabel had a brief, restrained encounter with a male friend of hers; let's call him Will. Isabel had a keen intuition for who was serious boyfriend material and who was in it just for sex or laughs. The latter would not do; only ardent, long-term devotion was of interest to her, and Will was clearly not about that. The evening after the encounter, she summoned him to her dorm room, sat him on her roommate's bed, and launched into the "it's not you, it's me" speech. As she talked on, she noticed Will's lips were twitching. *Does he find this funny?* she wondered, a bit miffed. Then she realized that blasting in through the window was the Rolling Stones song that goes, in part: "I'm so hot for her, I'm so hot for her, I'm so hot for her and SHE'S SO COLD."

Earlier that day, it transpired, Will (knowing Isabel's habits) had told some of his buddies on the hall what was likely to go down. They'd rigged up stereo speakers in order to prank him when the moment came. As Mick Jagger warbled on, Will started to laugh out loud. After a few moments of confused irritation, Isabel saw the joke and began to laugh, too.

Snow Queens may be chilly, but they are not without a sense of humor.

A decade later, Isabel wound up at the same company where I worked (the corporate training firm). She started as a copyeditor and within a few years had become a project manager and writer on the product development team. An extreme introvert, she was nervous about public speaking, but she saw that the people who advanced at the firm were those who taught—or "facilitated," as the jargon had it—workshops for clients. She resolved to do at least some facilitation but knew she would need to build her confidence. In true Snow-Queen style, she sat down and had a long think about how she might manage it. Finally she decided she would simply prepare more and better than anyone else. *I know how to prepare*, she thought, *so I'll rely on that.* For the next eighteen years as she climbed the ranks to become, ultimately, a member of the executive team, she over-prepared for every workshop, every presentation, and every speech, writing out copious notes and rehearsing in front of a mirror. She never lost her stage fright, but she did gain skill. Her hard work was rewarded one day when, after a talk to a London audience about a book she had coauthored, she was approached by the UK head of Sales who hugged her and said admiringly, "Best speaker at the company, hands down."

In 2006, Isabel won an award for Manager of the Year and another for leading the development of some new products. One of her nominations read:

It was a challenging year, with a lot of change and turmoil, yet [Isabel] showed steadfast leadership in setting [company] direction. She continued to steer a steady course even when the wind changed direction and the waves surged. She addressed each business challenge with focus, attention, and good humor.

Another person wrote, "There were many challenges along the way—pilots canceled, changes in team members—all of which she handled calmly and efficiently." A few years later, she received another nomination with this: "Her high degree of personal integrity and her calm, direct leadership was a beacon in the darkness of 2009." *Calm* was a word one heard often in connection with Isabel. Any of the archetypes can be an excellent leader, but none is as cool-headed in her leadership as a Snow Queen.

Sometimes, of course, the coolness can backfire. I recall one time when Isabel, fresh from running a meeting in which two of her team members had quarreled, decided the best thing to do would be to sit down right away with the two, plus another manager, and hash it out—calmly. The scene unfolded with one of the employees, a Snow Queen-Empress type, growing upset and angry at being (she thought) publicly chastised; the other employee, a male Amiga-Empath, settling in for a nice long talk about feelings but becoming increasingly perturbed when he saw his colleague's distress; and the manager, an Escapist, at a complete loss and desperate to leave the room. Isabel realized later how obtuse she had been. Since she herself generally had no difficulty keeping her balance in emotionally turbulent situations, the danger of throwing others off balance with her actions did not occur to her any more than it had occurred to her back in her days of college hookups and breakups.

But in general, her calm paid off, as you can tell from her award nominations. Her team members saw her as a rock, her colleagues as a trusted adviser, her bosses as a sharp yet reliable producer. Early in her career, someone said of her, "You talk softly, but carry a big stick." She liked that description a lot better than "dull cookie."

◆ ◆ ◆

I suppose it must be obvious by now that "Isabel" is me. As I've said, my principal archetype is the Snow Queen, and it is the Snow Queen's strengths that I've leaned on to get me through all sorts of difficult situations. At the same time, it is the Snow Queen's weaknesses that have often landed me *in* those difficult situations in the first place. It was pride, for example, that in 1992 led me to quit my job in a huff in order to take another job that, as should have been obvious, was a bad fit for me; and it was hubris, twenty years later, that pushed me into Medusa territory when my colleagues and I turned against our boss, Victor, with initially good but ultimately disastrous results (see the opening chapter).

Still, the high, cold, airy ways have on the whole served me well, as one more nomination letter may show:

> It was a horrible, no-good, very bad year … and we not only survived but also somehow thrived. Only it's not "somehow"; it's Jocelyn. She was a beacon of light in the fog, or maybe that long pole that tightrope walkers have to carry to keep from falling into the abyss. I'm not sure—some very strong metaphor, in any case. She was clear, thoughtful, endlessly supportive, and managed to balance keeping us on task, focusing us on the future, and allowing us room to breathe.

Learning from the Snow Queen

Reductive stereotypes are applied to the Snow Queen nearly as much as to the Temptress. A Snow Queen, in most men's minds, is a frigid bitch; as usual, though, the real picture is much more complex. To take advantage of the Snow Queen's strengths, follow this advice:

Expect commitment. Many people thought that I (a.k.a. Isabel) had success with college boys because of my looks or my touch-me-not air, but neither of those things was it. I got commitment thanks to one simple reason: I would stand for nothing less. If I hooked up with a guy and the next day he made it clear that, to him, the liaison had been just temporary fun, I brushed him off like a bumblebee and turned my attention elsewhere. My motto was "Sign on or begone." The soundtrack in my head was not "Will you still love me tomorrow?" but "Any man of mine better walk the line." Like Isolde, I was all in and expected my Tristan to be all in, too.

This is a good principle not just for romance, but also for social and professional life. The Snow Queen, being a focused type who takes her commitments (if not always herself) seriously, has no patience for those who regularly drop the ball or fail to follow through. It's good to show understanding toward a friend who forgets a phone chat or an employee who misses a deadline because of a family emergency, but if you're tolerating that type of behavior constantly, stop. Don't waste time with folks who are only going to waste it for you.

Focus on results. When it came to my team working remotely, I had a line I'd picked up from a former boss: "I don't care if you're in the office, at home, or floating in a pool on a purple dinosaur. I care about results." Years later, my ex-employees still talk about the purple dinosaur. They appreciated the statement because it made them feel trusted and that they could be themselves. They knew their personality and presence were, for me, secondary to their responsiveness, their reliability, and the results they achieved.

One of the big traps into which even seasoned leaders tend to fall is the abandonment-micromanagement trap. People placed in manager roles are typically high performers used to excelling on their own, so when they get promoted they continue in that mode, focusing on their own goals and paying little attention to their team (abandonment). Then, when things start to go awry, they panic and swoop in to meddle in every project, issue instructions for the smallest tasks, and try to change people's natures (micromanagement).

A Snow Queen rarely falls into this trap. She has no desire to poke her nose in anyone's business, but neither does she fear being in charge; so, she stays above the fray, dropping a word of advice here, a mild rebuke there, a bit of encouragement when needed. And, as long as the results are good, she doesn't care whether someone is sitting in the office, working from home, or floating on a purple dinosaur.

Keep calm and carry on. This stock phrase from World War II Britain is the Snow Queen's mantra. Take Isolde: she's passionate, but hardly a panicker. On the ship she is especially cool when calling upon Brangäne to provide the death draught and, later, persuading Tristan to drink it. When she arrives in Cornwall (we read in the *Romance*), she has no trouble controlling her illicit infatuation well enough to marry the king, conceal her feelings for months, and remain sexually faithful to her husband even after she and Tristan have been forced to flee into the forest. And she keeps calm and carries on (I have argued) even after her lover's death.

We underestimate the power of calm, not only on ourselves but on others. To quote Court Chilton, a consultant and instructor at MIT's Sloan Business School whom I interviewed for one of my previous books:

> Eighty percent of influence is managing your own reactions to other people. You have to influence yourself. If you can hang in while the storms rage, that is a form of influence. They'll say, "That person has an even keel. The wind blows harder, but they keep going. I want to be like that."[10]

If you are a Snow Queen, some will denounce you as dull or uptight. Most people, however, will appreciate your quiet strength. When storms rage, they'll look to you, the one with the cool head and the aerial view, for leadership.

PART FOUR

AIR-FIRE

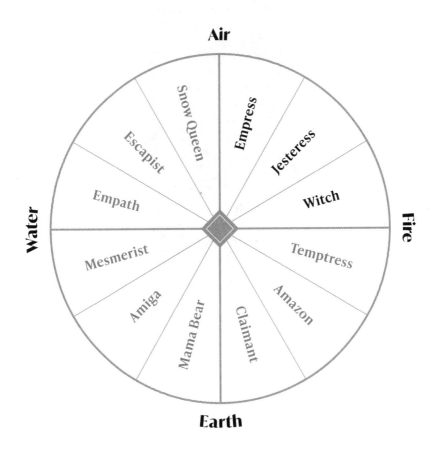

Air

Snow Queen

Empress

Escapist

Jesteress

Empath

Witch

Water

Fire

Mesmerist

Temptress

Amiga

Amazon

Mama Bear

Claimant

Earth

10

THE EMPRESS

THE THANE'S LADY, ALONE IN the dark Scottish castle, paces the room as she reads the letter aloud to herself. Her husband writes of his recent meeting with three witches in a wood:

> When I burnt in desire to question them further, they made themselves air, into which they vanished. Whiles I stood rapt in the wonder of it came missives [that is, messengers] from the King, who all-hailed me "Thane of Cawdor," by which title, before, the weird sisters saluted me, and referred me to the coming on of time with "Hail, king that shalt be!" This have I thought good to deliver thee, my dearest partner of greatness . . . Lay it to thy heart, and farewell. (*Macbeth*, act 1, scene 5)[1]

The lady folds up the letter and contemplates the situation.

Her husband is Thane of Glamis, a minor fief. Now, having fought beside the king to suppress the Thane of Cawdor's rebellion (or was it just Cawdor's growing power and popularity?) Glamis has been rewarded with that title, too, and is lord of a much larger province. This is good news indeed, but it comes with a big drawback: he is kinsman to King Duncan, so his elevation will give him some claim to the throne of Scotland—or at least, the king might come to think so. If so, the new Thane of Glamis and Cawdor could be the next man with his head on a pike, no matter what the witches said.

In his letter, he calls his wife his "partner of greatness." But she knows she is more than a partner; she is the greater of the two, in intelligence, ambition, strategy, foresight, and resolve. Her husband is "too full o' the milk of human kindness…What thou wouldst highly," she muses, "that wouldst thou holily."(1.5) To be blunt, he is weak. If they are to make it through this political mire alive and take the crown seemingly given him by fate, she will need to pour her spirits in his ear, stiffen his spine, and do most of the thinking for him.

A messenger arrives with the news that King Duncan is coming to stay with them that very night. The lady puts away the letter and begins to prepare.

Lady Macbeth: The Unsexed Queen

We are now in the realm of air and fire; of brilliant, combustible women who soar like shooting stars but often come in for harsh condemnation, even unto death: think Anne Boleyn, executed by order of her husband, Henry VIII; Hypatia of Alexandria, the greatest mathematician and astronomer of her time, killed by a mob of religious zealots; and Daenerys Targaryen, the *Game of Thrones* mother of dragons, slain by her lover-rival. These women are not snow and mist, but lightning storms; not volcanoes, but fireworks.

The Empress is denounced as overbearing, overambitious, and (horror of horrors) unfeminine. Only her sister the Witch is more reviled; even the Amazon is praised as strong and sexy. Shakespeare's Lady Macbeth—who in a famous soliloquy calls upon the "spirits that tend on mortal thoughts" to "unsex me here" and "come to my woman's breasts and take my milk for gall" (1.5)—is known as drama's ultimate evil queen, largely because she is the one who drives her husband to assassinate King Duncan, thereby committing the sin not only of guest-murder but also of henpecking. But an Empress will never sit back when a prize is at hand and her partner incapable of seizing it. She is, as I've said before, the most masculine of the archetypes; that is, the most manlike in her enthusiasm for climbing ladders political, social, or corporate. And when the men are ineffectual (as they mostly are in this play), the Empress **takes charge**. She is like one of those fish that change from female to male when circumstances demand it.

Lady Macbeth barely puts up a pretense of subservience to her husband. Having received the report that the king will be staying with them that night and knowing it's now or never, she welcomes Macbeth home with a few flattering words ("Great Glamis! Worthy Cawdor! Greater than both by the all-hail hereafter!"), then immediately shifts to lecturing him. "Your face is as a book," she says. *Don't be so obvious. Hide your feelings. Act normal. And for Pete's sake, don't try to manage this affair*:

> You shall put
> This night's great business into my dispatch,
> Which shall to all our nights and days to come
> Give solely sovereign sway and masterdom. (1.5)

Note how she includes herself in the anticipated masterdom. Macbeth doesn't argue with her, saying only that they'll discuss it further, but she continues to press, warning him again to greet the king calmly. Her last words in the scene are, "Leave all the rest to me."

The Empress's way of persuasion is not the indirect way of the Amiga or Mesmerist. She does not cajole, distract, or negotiate; she **insists**. And if her target will not comply, she escalates to mocking, to berating, even to emotional blackmail. When Lady Macbeth sees her husband still hesitating, she flings this at him:

> Was the hope drunk
> Wherein you dressed yourself? Hath it slept since?
> And wakes it now, to look so green and pale
> At what it did so freely? From this time

Such I account thy love. Art thou afeared
To be the same in thine own act and valor
As thou art in desire . . .
Letting "I dare not" wait upon "I would,"
Like the poor cat i' the adage? (1.7)

The adage in question is, "The cat would eat fish, and would not wet her feet." Lady Macbeth is essentially calling her spouse a pussy.

She asks why he even raised the possibility of murdering Duncan if he didn't intend to do it, thereby letting us know it was he, not she, who had the idea in the first place and who now lacks the guts to follow through. "When you durst do it, then you were a man," she sneers. Macbeth must wince at the jab, but she drives the knife in deeper:

I have given suck, and know
How tender 'tis to love the babe that milks me;
I would, while it was smiling in my face,
Have plucked my nipple from his boneless gums
And dashed his brains out, had I so sworn as you
Have done to this. (1.7)

Macbeth is still unsure. "If we should fail?" he quavers.

"We fail?" she replies—which could mean "Then we fail; so what?" or "Us, fail?" But they *won't* fail, she says, as long as he keeps his head, screws his courage to the sticking place, and above all, heeds her directions. Macbeth is persuaded, at least for the moment. He says to her with admiration, "Bring forth men-children only, for thy undaunted mettle should compose nothing but males." He approves her plan to drug the wine of Duncan's chamberlains and frame them for the murder by wiping their clothes with the bloody dagger. Finally he says, "I am settled, and bend up each corporal agent to this terrible feat."

The Empress is good at taking the lead and insisting that people follow her. The other thing she's good at is **compartmentalizing**. Lady Macbeth has already welcomed King Duncan to the castle with every appearance of a gracious hostess and loyal servant, showing no sign of what she has in mind. Now, in the middle of the night, she waits calmly, even eagerly, while her husband sets off to do the murder. Hearing noises, she wonders if the grooms have wakened. *Dammit*, she thinks; *I laid the daggers ready for him. I should have done the job myself. I would have, if only Duncan hadn't looked so much like my father as he slept.*

But soon Macbeth appears, carrying the bloody daggers. His face is pale, his eyes wild. "This is a sorry sight," he says, staring at his hands.

"A foolish thought, to say a sorry sight," his wife replies, and when he describes voices howling that he'll never sleep again, she tries to soothe him as a mother soothes a fretful child: "Why, worthy thane, you do unbend your noble strength to think so brainsickly of things. Go get some water and wash this filthy witness from your hand." (2.2) She chides him for bringing the daggers and tells him to go back, leave them by the grooms as planned, but he won't do it; he will not look upon the dreadful deed he can't stop thinking about. She loses patience:

> Infirm of purpose!
> Give me the daggers. The sleeping and the dead
> Are but as pictures. 'Tis the eye of childhood
> That fears a painted devil. If he do bleed,
> I'll gild the faces of the grooms withal
> For it must seem their guilt. (2.2)

After she leaves the room, he crumbles: "How is 't with me, when every noise appalls me? What hands are here? Ha! They pluck out mine eyes. Will all great Neptune's ocean wash this blood clean from my hand?" *No*, he whispers; *rather, my hand will redden the ocean.*

His wife reenters, cool as stone. "My hands are of your color," she says, "but I shame to wear a heart so white . . . Retire we to our chamber. A little water clears us of this deed." The contrast is striking: To him, the whole world is stained with guilt, indelible, inescapable. To her, the guilt may be washed away as easily as a drop of meat juice.

Once she is crowned, however, she finds the deed not so easily compart-mented. She begins to sleepwalk, causing her gentlewoman to call in a doctor to observe her strange behavior. This is the famous "Out, damned spot" scene (5.1), wherein Queen Macbeth wanders about in the middle of the night, eyes open but sightless, rubbing her hands as if trying to wash them clean. "Yet who would have thought the old man to have had so much blood in him? . . . Here's the smell of blood still . . . O, O, O!" she cries.

The doctor, after watching her for a time, says her mind is diseased—and indeed, most directors have the actress play the character as insane or on the way to it. But we should observe that her bursts of distress ("Will these hands ne'er be clean?") are outnumbered by remarks such as these: "Fie, my lord, fie, a soldier, and afeared? What need we fear who knows it, when none can call our power to account?" "No more o' that, my lord, no more o' that; you mar all with this starting." "Come, come . . . give me your hand. What's done cannot be undone." It's my view that Lady Macbeth's madness tends to be overplayed; she may be feeling the horror of the murder, but a close reading of the scene reveals that her Empress-like abilities to take charge, insist on obedience, and put worries aside are still very much intact.

In the end she commits suicide (so they say), and her husband is over-thrown by Duncan's son Malcolm, who has made a deal with England's king in exchange for an army. Malcolm promotes all the thanes to earls, promising better times now that Scotland is free of the "dead butcher and his fiendlike queen." In short, things don't work out for the Macbeths. And likely they deserve the epithets.

Shakespeare's audience, however, would have been aware that no English king was ever a friend to the Scots; moreover, they would surely have wondered about the new-made *earls* and how pleased they really were to be "honored" with an English title. I've already suggested that Lady Macbeth foresaw her husband's downfall once Duncan had raised him high. Did she also foresee what would happen to Scotland should Malcolm, England's puppet, inherit the throne? Did she perceive a competence vacuum created by weak men and seek to fill it by putting herself in power by proxy? Maybe she was a fiend. Or maybe, she was an Empress whose well-laid plans gang agley, destroyed by a husband who couldn't keep up.

Amanda: Building Empires

I've mentioned Amanda before. She started at our company as a customer service representative and rose, over the course of twenty years, from account executive to regional vice president to head of Global Sales. She had a Manhattanite's fast walk and penchant for black clothing, though she eventually acquired a second home in the Massachusetts countryside where she would preside over offsite meetings with her sales force. The impression that she would bulldoze anyone who got in her or her team's way earned her many loyal fans and a few vehement detractors, but no one ever questioned her right to be at the top.

Our company had sales-job applicants take a personality-and-aptitude assessment from an outside firm. Managers were also allowed to take it for their own enlightenment; I myself took it when I joined the executive team, whereupon I learned, among other things, that I was in the first percentile—as low as one can get—on "sociability." The coach who walked me through my results was a bit shocked: "Ha-ha, we rarely see a score *that* low!" he exclaimed, then seemed to recall himself and reassured me I was not a freak. (I, as the Snow Queen, was quite pleased to have my outstanding anti-sociability confirmed.) We then talked about another factor on which I had scored low: ego-drive. This, said the coach, was the desire to persuade. He went on to say that a strong ego-drive was deemed a key success factor for sales reps at our firm, and he cited Amanda as a preeminent example: "She scored extremely high on that one," he said. Although I was surprised at his somewhat unprofessional revealing of another employee's results, I was not at all surprised to learn that Amanda's ego-drive was off the charts.

I remember a time when I joined her and one of her employees, a young man named Carl who was just starting out in sales, for a pitch to a big pharmaceutical company. It went well, the client all but giving us the nod as we left, and as we sat in a restaurant afterward having a late lunch, Carl said, "That was fun."

Amanda's face lit up. She leaned forward. "I know, wasn't it? It's the greatest feeling. And now that you've done it, you'll want to do it again and again. You'll never want to stop."

I listened, baffled. All I'd felt was relief that the stressful meeting was over, and here Amanda was talking about it as if it had been an episode of mind-blowing sex.

The Empress shares with the Mesmerist a desire and ability to influence—that is, to change another's mind and actions—but unlike the Mesmerist, she doesn't do it in a subtle way and doesn't have patience for the long game. Amanda came straight at you with an arsenal of smiles, good reasons, a sense of urgency, and sheer force of personality, so that you felt she was making you an offer you couldn't refuse. Cheryl, the five-million-dollar woman of chapter 6, disguised her efforts to have her way, veiling them in her wish to serve the client. Amanda threw no such veil over her intent. She was most comfortable in a position of authority, hence was actually a better sales manager than a salesperson. As a salesperson, you can't control a lot; moreover, the pace of decisions, set by the customer, is often frustratingly slow. Amanda liked to be in control, and as I've said, she liked to move fast. Cheryl the Mesmerist, if you resisted her plans, would keep talking: she would flatter, reassure, ask your advice, and convey her excitement until finally you found yourself agreeing. Amanda the Empress, if you dared say "No," would simply hang up. Then she'd go find someone else to do her will.

Amanda's dominance at the company sometimes infuriated me. I recall one senior management meeting at which we were to discuss new structures for each function. I came prepared to present my proposed org chart for R&D; when my turn arrived, however, our president, Bob, looked at me and said, "May I?" He rose, went to the whiteboard, and began to talk through *his* ideas for *my* team. I was miffed but said nothing, figuring maybe he was going to do the same for everyone—after all, he was the boss—and once he'd finished with my group, I waited for him to launch into his plan for Sales. But instead he handed the marker to Amanda, sat down, and proceeded to listen with apparent approval as she gave her own spiel. Enraged, I clenched my toes inside my shoes. Had Amanda arranged it in advance? Or had Bob just naturally deferred to her? I didn't know then, and still don't know.

Later that week, I told a friend about the incident. "Why did she get to present her structure and I got mine presented to me?" I huffed.

"I bet Bob's intimidated by her," my friend said. "I mean, she's the man in that room."

My friend was right: Amanda was The Man in every room. And she achieved that status not just thanks to her ego-drive—which women may possess as much as men—but also as a result of two other attributes, both of which are more typically masculine than feminine.

The first was her absolute acceptance of hierarchy. As I said at the start of this book, men are comfortable saluting captains; women, far less so. At our firm, it was always women leading the revolution—but never Amanda. When pushed to the brink she might join in with after-hours kvetching about management; in the office, though, she wouldn't so much as roll her eyes. Unfailingly deferential to her superiors, she toed the line while at the same time pressing hard for what she wanted and, if denied her way, backing off and biding her time until the boss had forgotten about it and she could forge ahead undeterred. When after 25 years of service she finally decided to take a new job, our group CEO—the same guy who had fired me a year or two earlier—gave her (so I heard) a nice sendoff with many expressions of gratitude. Amanda played it the company way and was rewarded with company laurels.

The second attribute that helped boost her to the top was her ability, like Lady Macbeth, to compartmentalize. No matter what was going down, Amanda could put extraneous concerns aside and focus on the task at hand. She prided herself on this skill. Say, for example, the CEO had given us all a tongue-lashing about the quarter's disappointing numbers. I would be thrown off for the rest of the day, if not the whole week; Amanda would simply pick up her Prada bag, ask her assistant to bring her a grande skim latte, and move on to her next meeting. I can imagine her chastising me in the words of the Scottish queen: "My hands are of your color, but I shame to wear a heart so white . . . Be not lost so poorly in your thoughts."

The Empress may be the most courageous of the archetypes. She has to be: reaching for the brass ring and missing it is her greatest fear, yet she can't bear *not* to reach for it. Unlike the Amazon, who is a happy warrior, the Empress is a worried striver. She puts herself out there time and again, seeking respect, dreading humiliation, and never feeling quite secure in her position.

When Amanda and I were just starting out, both in our mid-twenties, we were assigned to a cross-functional team whose mission was to improve how orders were fulfilled. After nearly a year of work, the team, which included a dozen people from multiple levels, was asked to share its results at an all-company meeting. Slated as presenters were three or four young employees; I was not one of them, for which I was thankful, and I took my seat in the auditorium hoping the session wouldn't take too long. A few minutes later, Amanda arrived and sat down two seats to my right. She, I knew, had volunteered to present, though she wasn't the first up.

I glanced at her. She had her feet wedged on the seatback in front, her knees crunched up to her chest, her hands cupped over her nose and mouth. As the first presenter was introduced and went through her piece with an air of natural confidence, Amanda remained rigid, staring straight ahead, white as a ghost.

When her turn finally came, she got up, marched down to the stage, and slayed it.

Two decades later, I mentioned the incident to her. "You looked absolutely terrified," I said, laughing at the thought of our now–Queen of Sales ever having been afraid of public speaking. "Do you remember?"

"I remember," she said. "You know where I'd been five minutes earlier?"

"No, where?"

"Outside, throwing up in the bushes."

I eyed her with new respect. And I recalled the old Spanish proverb: *With the rich and mighty, always a little patience.*

Learning from the Empress

The Empress is the foremost example of the woman who sits at the table, plays hardball, and in all respects follows the advice offered by the "lean in" advocates. Here are four ways to channel this archetype.

Respect the hierarchy. I'll say it again: men tend to feel at home in pyramids, women not so much. To be an Empress, you need to get comfortable operating within a chain of command.

One way to do this is to understand what men mean when they say, "Be a team player." To most women, a team player is someone who collaborates with, helps, and supports her colleagues. If our boss accuses us of not being a team player, we're confused: Are we not helpful? Are we not supportive? We fail to grasp that for men, a team player is someone who supports the team *captain.* It doesn't matter how nice you are to your peers; if you defy your boss—or worse, make him look bad—you are not a team player, and you will suffer the consequences. Amanda understood this. Though she wasn't always popular with her peers, she made sure always to be popular with her boss, her boss's boss, and so on up the ladder. As a result, she got a hand up at every rung.

Speak with conviction. The main complaint men make about women in the workplace is that we take too long to get to the point. While this criticism isn't entirely fair—what about men's poor listening skills?—it isn't entirely unfair, either. As girls, we are taught to soften our speech: to hesitate, to apologize, to engage in "up-talk" (raising our tone at the end of a sentence as if asking a question), and to wrap our statements in *maybes* and *I'm-not-sures*: "Sorry if I misunderstood you ... um ... I'm not really sure about this, but I think, maybe, there might be another way to look at it?" We also overuse the word *just*: "It's just that I noticed a few minor problems with the prototype." "I just wanted to see how you're coming along with that report." These speech patterns make us sound weak, indecisive, and deserving of Lady Macbeth's rebuke: *Be not lost so poorly in your thoughts.*

An Empress keeps her remarks short and definite, with no ifs, buts, or justs:

"Here's another way to look at it." "I saw three problems in the prototype." "Please have the report to me by end of day Tuesday." Moreover, she knows the power of silence and uses it to her advantage.

Push for your purpose. Amanda's ego-drive may have caused her to come across as bossy, but it also propelled her rise. She was rarely ill-humored or rude; she did not hesitate, however, to make her desires and opinions known, nor did she disguise her eagerness to persuade you to her side. As I said in the Amazon chapter, many women have a hard time articulating even to themselves what they want. The Empress not only knows what she wants, she states it out loud and maintains that you should want it, too.

If this sounds too aggressive, start small. The next time someone asks your opinion on a trivial matter—where to go for lunch, say—don't reply with, "Oh, I don't mind, wherever you want to go"; instead say, "I really like Josie's Café, how about there?" When someone praises you for your accomplishment, don't hand the credit to another; instead say, "Thank you, I'm very proud of the work." Avoid apologizing unless you truly did something wrong. And, when someone disagrees with your point of view, don't rush to back down; stand your ground with, "I hear you, and I see it differently; here's why."

Lean in—literally. Ambitious women, unlike ambitious men, are often perceived as dislikable. This unfortunate fact is one side of the so-called tightrope dilemma I described earlier: come on too strong, you're a bitch; come on too soft, you're a doormat. Research summarized in *What Works for Women at Work*, by Joan C. Williams and Rachel Dempsey, indicates that a sociable style—outgoing, animated, pleasant—works better than a submissive, reserved, or domineering style when it comes to walking the tightrope. As you lean in figuratively, you can avoid being disliked if you also lean in literally, signaling "friendly" with your body language and tone.

Sit up tall. Uncross your arms. Tilt your torso forward. Speak with energy. Nod.

And above all, as you make your Empress deals and lay your Empress plans: smile!

◇ **11** ◇

THE JESTERESS

IN TADANOBU'S NIGHT-WATCH ROOM, half a dozen dapper young gentlemen are relaxing over rice wine and reminiscing about women. Tadanobu, a senior courtier known for his poetic skill, is talking of Sei Shonagon, a lady in the Empress's service who was once a friend—a very *close* friend—but who fell out with him over political opinions. Now whenever he passes her door, he lifts his sleeve to avoid even glancing in her direction.

"I've been waiting vainly in hopes she might send word of some sort," Tadanobu is saying in a tone half-cross, half-amused, "and I just hate the way she seems to shrug the whole thing off without a thought, and simply ignores me. Why don't we test her once and for all tonight?"[1]

The other men, chuckling and nodding, scoot closer. Putting their heads together, they come up with a line from Bo Juyi, a famous Chinese poet: "You are there in the flowering capital / beneath the Council Chamber's brocade curtains." Tadanobu scribes it with care on thin blue paper. Then he adds: "How should it end, tell me?"[2]

He folds up the paper, summons a messenger and sends him off, instructing him to bring the letter back should there be no reply. The men refill their cups and sit back, grinning. "We've got her this time," says one. "The cleverest lady in the world wouldn't be up to this challenge!"

Sei Shonagon: A Battle of Wits

"A thousand years ago," writes translator Meredith McKinney, "a lady at the imperial court of Japan settled herself in front of a precious bundle of paper and began to write the extraordinary work called *Makura no sōshi*, known to English readers as *The Pillow Book*."[3]

The lady, Sei Shonagon,* was born around 966. She had been married, but the marriage ended in divorce, and in her late twenties she entered the service of the Empress Teishi. Along with perhaps two dozen other gentlewomen, Sei had the job of keeping the young empress entertained and bringing credit to her household; of enhancing, as the Victorians might say, the reputation of her salon. Medieval Japan's high society was supremely aesthetic; never before or after has there been a world in which people took so seriously painting, music, dress, calligraphy, interior decor, landscaping, and above all, poetry. Yet *seriously* is the wrong word, for to be thought plodding or dull was the worst fate imaginable. If a person was to have any standing in that rarefied milieu, he or she must have wit—the sparkling wit of the Jesteress.

Like all Japanese upper-class women of the era, the empress and her ladies lived lives of strict seclusion. Officially, face-to-face interactions with the opposite sex were limited to husbands and other relatives; unofficially, male lovers could make nighttime visits, as long as they left before dawn's light allowed them to see their paramour clearly. During the day, flirtations were carried out through curtains, standing screens, or hanging blinds, with only the woman's long, layered, multicolored silk sleeves protruding gracefully under the barrier as evidence of her taste—regarded as more important than

---

* Tradition has it that her personal name was Nagiko. *Sei* was her family name, and *Shonagon* meant something like "junior counselor," following the custom of calling ladies by the title of a male relative.

her beauty. The middle classes, it seems, thought court ladies a bit slutty; in her book, Sei scoffs at the provincials' inability to appreciate the graceful arts of romance as practiced by the higher ranks.

The Pillow Book, however, is not (as its title might suggest) a book about sex. It is, rather, a sort of blog: a personal collection of anecdotes, lists, musings, and opinions, all revolving on the theme of *okashi*, meaning that which amuses, intrigues, charms, or delights. A pillow book was a journal to keep bedside, ready to receive one's thoughts. Paper was expensive and hard to come by, so a bundle of scrolls was a lavish gift. Sei reports that when a palace minister presented such a bundle to the empress, Her Majesty wondered aloud what to do with it.

"They are copying the *Records of the Historian* over at His Majesty's court," says the Empress, using for *copying* the idiom *laying out bedding*.

"This should be a 'pillow,' then," Sei suggests. A pillow to compete with a bed.

"Very well," says Her Majesty, smiling as she hands it over, "it's yours."

Why give the paper to Sei? Because Empress Teishi knows her position is in peril: her powerful father has died, her brother is in exile, and the emperor has taken a second wife. A book from her salon, a marvelous book to amuse and delight, will be just the thing to boost her status. Sei Shonagon, as the most erudite and witty of her ladies, is the one to write it.

And indeed, *The Pillow Book* ended up going viral, courtiers tussling to get hold of a copy. Although it didn't help Empress Teishi—who died after childbirth at age 23, her status never restored—Sei's book is still in print more than a millennium later.

The Jesteress, our eleventh archetype, is no fool. She is funny, occasionally even clownish, but unlike the blunt, earthy humor of the Temptress, her humor has a sharp, shining edge, an edge she uses to disarm and diminish her adversaries. Let's return to Tadanobu's poetry challenge (one of many such anecdotes in the book) and see how Sei the Jesteress uses her **rapier wit** to defeat the ex-lover hoping to embarrass her.

It's pouring that evening, and the Empress's gentlewomen are gathered around a lamp playing a writing game when a maid enters to announce the arrival of a message for Sei. The messenger says he was instructed by Secretary Captain Tadanobu to give Sei the letter personally, so she goes out to the veranda, and he passes it under the straw blind. "Considering how Tadanobu hates me," she thinks, "what can he have written?" Feeling nervous, she tells the messenger to be off, she'll send a reply later. She returns to the game, tucking the note away.

But before long, back he comes. "The Secretary Captain has said that if there is no reply I'm to bring back his letter. Do be quick."[4] His voice is testy. He's getting soaked.

Even more nervous now, Sei unfolds the paper. She reads the line from poet Bo Juyi: "You are there in the flowering capital / beneath the Council Chamber's brocade curtains." And underneath, Tadanobu's challenge: "How should it end, tell me?"

"What on earth shall I do?" she wonders.

At this point we must pause to understand the context for this linguistic tennis match. First, Japanese gentlemen of the era wrote in Chinese, their education having been devoted largely to the Chinese classics. Quite a few ladies also knew the language and the books, but it was not thought ladylike to demonstrate this knowledge; women had their own Japanese script, called *kana*, which they used to write memoirs, arrange trysts, and share news with friends.* A lady receiving a line of Chinese poetry could neither reveal that she knew the rest of the actual poem nor reply in Chinese characters. To do so would be thought dreadfully crass.

Second, the poetic game was played for high stakes. Men and women alike were expected to have memorized—and were tested on—large collections of Japanese poetry, which, along with the Chinese collections, were the foundation for most social discourse. McKinney writes:

> Anyone who hoped to be admired and accepted had to be deeply
> knowledgeable about the poetic canon . . . and able to weave appro-
> priate allusions [to those poems] into her or his own occasional

---

* *The Pillow Book* was written in kana.

poetry. Wittily nuanced messages, generally containing a poem, flew constantly between members of the court and sometimes beyond; these in turn required a suitable extempore poem in response, written in an elegant hand on paper carefully chosen for appropriateness of color and quality, in every aspect of which one's sensibility and character would be displayed for intense scrutiny.[5]

Given this scrutiny and the no-Chinese-for-ladies rule, it's no wonder Sei is anxious. But the messenger is urging her to hurry, so she grabs a piece of dead charcoal from the brazier and writes at the end of the letter, in Japanese kana script: "Who will come visiting / this grass-thatched hut?" The messenger carries it away. She waits for a reply, but none comes. Eventually she shrugs and heads for bed in her own quarters.

Early next morning, she hears a gentleman outside calling in grandiose tones: "Is 'Grass-thatched Hut' present?"

Sei goes out to the veranda to receive him. "What on earth?" she says through the blinds. "Why should you think anyone with such a depressing name might be here?"[6]

The gentleman is a friend of Tadanobu's, and he proceeds to fill her in on what happened in the night-watch room the previous evening. It seems the men were congratulating themselves on their poetic slam-dunk when back came the messenger with Sei's reply. Tadanobu opened the letter, stared, and cried, "Oh! How extraordinary! Whatever's this?"

The men gathered round to look. Gasps of admiration ensued. "What a clever rogue she is! No, you really can't give her up!"[7]

They tried to supply the first three lines of the new poem (the next move in the game), but racked their brains for hours to no avail, says Tadanobu's friend. "We decided it would make a fine tale for future telling, at any rate." He takes his leave with a bow.

Sei is pondering how awful it will be to go down in history with such a name attached, when Norimitsu, her ex-husband—by convention now known as her "brother"—arrives all in a tizzy: "My dear, I've been looking for you to express my heartfelt joy at the wonderful news!"

"What wonderful news?" Sei asks. "Have you been given a new post?"

"No, no, I could barely wait to congratulate you on the wonderful thing that happened last night! There couldn't be a greater honor!"

He proceeds to tell her the same story all over again. When the men received Sei's reply, he says, everyone was full of praise. "Come over here, Sei's Brother," they urged. "Come and hear this!" They worked long into the night trying to complete the poem, finally agreeing that it would look worse if they sent something unimpressive, "...so it all petered out in defeat," says Norimitsu. "This is a most wonderful thing for us both, don't you think? Far more cause for celebration than receiving some trifling post!"[8]

Sei just has time to marvel that her ex is being called "Sei's Brother" rather than his proper title, when a summons arrives from the empress. She, too, wants to talk about the "grass-thatched hut." It turns out that the emperor himself heard the story and laughed about it. "All the gentlemen have written your reply on their fans," says Her Majesty.

Why is this incident such a big deal? Here's why:

The Bo Juyi poem in full reads, "You are there in the flowering capital / beneath the Council Chamber's brocade curtains / while I sit on a rainy night / in my grass-thatched hut beneath Lu Shan mountain."[9] Sei knows the poem but, for reasons explained above, cannot respond in Chinese; moreover, simply to add the next line would be poor show. Instead, she creates the last two lines of a new poem—"Who will come visiting / this grass-thatched hut?"—which (a) demonstrates with graceful obliqueness that she knows the original poem very well; (b) alludes to Tadanobu's discourteous failure to call on her; and (c) is written in charcoal, suggesting a humble life in a rustic hut. It's an aesthetic tour de force in eight short words. And it seals her triumph: not only do her words decorate the men's fans, but from then on, she says, "Tadanobu no longer raised that shielding sleeve when we met."

This anecdote, along with many of the stories in *The Pillow Book*, reveals two more Jesteress qualities besides rapier wit. One, she **plays the game**. Sei could have ignored Tadanobu's letter: "After all," she might have reasoned, "he's only trying to bait me." Plus, it's cold, dark, and wet on the veranda: much easier to shoo away the messenger and go back inside where it's warm.

Despite all that, Sei steps up and takes a swing. No pen? No problem. She'll improvise with charcoal. No time to reflect? OK, she'll write the first thing that comes to mind, and she'll throw in a subtle jab at Tadanobu's bad manners while she's at it.

Two, she is **mistress of the humble-brag**. Japanese culture, then even more than now, demanded that women (especially) be self-deprecating, but Sei manages to highlight the audacity of her achievement nonetheless. "When I contemplated how innocent I'd been of involvement in the plot," she writes, "it made me nervous to think how easily I could have disgraced myself." And later, when she thinks about her line on the fans: "I was amazed, and could only wonder what had possessed me to make me produce such a brilliant response."[10]

A brilliant, laughing star, sparkling in the rain: that's the Jesteress.

Zara: Everyone Has to Be Teased

My mother's name—her real name—was Zara. Throughout her life she drew upon many of the archetypes as she traveled the world with my father, a career diplomat. At any given hour one could find her almost anywhere on the wheel: Empress, Amiga, Mama Bear, Temptress . . . she could have been a Bond girl, says my brother. But her primary archetype was the Jesteress.

She had a motto she'd pull out whenever one of her children was sniveling about a verbal poke: "Everyone has to be teased," she'd say, with a smile and a raise of her thick eyebrows. That usually stopped the sniveling, for we knew she meant *everyone*: children, grownups, herself included. We also knew she wasn't talking about real bullying (which she did not tolerate), but about the friendly mockery that adds spice to life, if only we know how to take it.

I was five when I first learned about April Fools' Day. Fascinated by the information and feeling very daring, I decided to test the concept. I stood at the living room window and called out, "Mummy! There's a big truck coming up the driveway!"

She came running from the kitchen. "What? I'm not expecting..." She peered out the window and stopped. There was no truck.

"April Fools!" I shouted, thrilled but also a little apprehensive. Would she be angry?

Her confused look changed to one of delight. She hugged me, laughing.

"Were you fooled?" I asked, bouncing on my toes. "Were you *really* fooled?"

"I was! I was completely fooled! How clever of you!" She hugged me again.

She loved games. On holidays or just regular days with the family gathered, she'd organize charades, hunt-the-thimble, board games, pencil-and-paper games, treasure hunts. One snowy afternoon when I was a teenager, she announced she was going sledding in the woods near our house. I had my doubts—well, she was *old*, in her 40s!—but they melted away when I saw her fling herself prone on the Flexible Flyer and go hurtling down the bumpy path, steering around trees like a champ. When we went on hikes she'd have us pretend we were Dorothy and friends in *The Wizard of Oz*. We'd chant "lions and tigers and bears, oh my!" as we tramped along, watching out for witches and flying monkeys. She knew how to short-sheet a bed; she used the British term "apple-pie bed," and I still remember, at age eight in my English grandmother's house, wondering why all the relatives had come to wish me good night and were standing in my bedroom doorway, grinning, and then that moment of shocked disorientation as my feet hit the folded sheet, followed by everyone, including me, dissolving in giggles.

Her wit, like Sei Shonagon's, could also have an edge. She was, as I've said, a foreign-service wife and went with her husband, my dad, to a new overseas post every few years. Needing to deal with all sorts of people in all sorts of unfamiliar situations, she used humor to navigate the sociocultural minefields. And she wrote about it, in numerous letters to family and friends. Her mother-in-law, having kept those letters—at least five hundred pages' worth—arranged for them to be typed up, copied, and bound as a gift to us grandchildren. *Letters from the Foreign Service* is my mother's pillow book, filled, like Sei's, with anecdotes, quips, and appreciation for okashi: the things that amuse and delight.

From October 1979 to September 1981, my father was stationed as US Ambassador to Guyana, the former British colony on the north coast of South America.* Early in their time there, my mother went to pay an official call on the wife of the Guyanese Prime Minister. One of her letters describes the visit:

A very amusing morning. My call had been arranged for 10:30. I arrived at [Prime Minister Burnham's] chained gate at 10:31. A very suspicious guard sloped up to the car window and said, "Huh?" Shepard (George's driver) said it was the wife of the American Ambassador to call on Mrs. Burnham. No answer. [The guard] sloped off to the house, leaving us sitting outside the locked gate. After a few minutes he signaled from the house to another guard that we could enter. We did.

I went up the stairs and was met by a secretary type who asked me to sit down and said that Mrs. Burnham would be right out. I sat. I waited. And waited. The room HIDEOUS, and not a book or magazine or anything to look at. The room opened onto a veranda on two sides, and I could see the Prime Minister sitting quietly in a corner doing some writing. His minions kept running back and forth to him. I waited. I decided I would wait 20 minutes, then I would leave my card and walk out. Politely. The Prime Minister kept peering around the corner at me. Finally, after 15 minutes or so, he pushed a bell, a minion ran to see what he wanted, a message was carried somewhere, and Mrs. Burnham appeared, apologizing. She and I then had a friendly, not exciting, conversation about I don't know what.

His granddaughter (about 4) and a small friend were running around, yelling and fighting. The Prime Minister kept getting up and coming into our room to tell the children to pipe down because

---

* Guyana's jungle interior was the site of the Jonestown massacre of November 1978, the aftermath of which became my father's challenge to cope with. Due to that terrible incident, along with the United States' lukewarm support of Guyana's socialist government, Americans were not popular there at the time.

he had to write his New Year's speech. He was introduced to me, and we passed pleasantries. I thought him charming.

An amusing exchange: The small friend of the granddaughter had lost his empty cigarette box and was trying to take the girl's. The Prime Minister told her that she ought to share it in the true Socialist Spirit. I suggested he cut it in half—but then they would both cry as neither would be satisfied. He then told the little friend that he could only get it if he were big enough to fight for it. I told the P.M. that was a horrible New Year's message to his granddaughter. Whereupon he looked at me and said that the world was a cruel place and the sooner they learned it, the better. I did NOT ask him where all his socialist/brotherly sentiments came into the picture!

I finally felt I'd spent quite long enough and left. Funny visit.[11]

In Zara's world, everyone had to be teased—even prime ministers.

In chapter 2 of this book I told of confronting my mother about her drinking habit, which for much of her life consisted of two double gin martinis per night. She took my words to heart and changed, dialing way back on the alcohol for her remaining seven years. At the time I credited myself for having the Amazonian courage to fight with good intent, but the truth is: her Jesteress sense of humor, along with the adaptability it fostered, deserves as much credit. Though taken aback by my mini-intervention, she didn't cry or rage; in fact, after a few minutes, she seemed to find it entertaining. And when I took my leave on that visit, she laughed as she kissed me and said, "Dear Joss! Thank you for looking after your annoying old parents."

The day she died, my brothers and I were at her bedside in the hospice facility. She was lucid but in and out of consciousness, made sleepy by the morphine. She woke up and asked for some orange juice; it was about ten a.m., and the cup was sitting on the tray table. My brother guided the straw to her lips.

"Ah, that's good," she said with eyes closed and a small sigh. "The two best things in life are the first sip of orange juice in the morning and the first sip of gin at night."

"Right!" we said, smiling at the familiar quip.

At her memorial gathering, we quoted that line. Intervention or no intervention, she got the last amusing word.

Learning from the Jesteress

My sense of fun, inherited from my mother, has saved me many a time from the traps to which a Snow Queen is liable. Uptight and unfriendly I may be, but I can take a joke—and dish one out. Here are three ways you too can call upon your inner Jesteress.

Take fights lightly. Along with the Temptress, the Jesteress is the first to laugh no matter how fraught the situation. Sei Shonagon had been snubbed and bad-mouthed by her ex-lover, an influential man, and she might naturally have lashed out in anger at his latest attempt to discredit her. Or, she might have taken the Escapist's route—which isn't a bad one—and simply ignored him, following Gavin de Becker's advice for women being pestered: "Best response? No response." But the Jesteress enjoys banter, and if you have this archetype in you, you probably can't always resist punching back. That's fine; the key is to punch back with good humor, thereby lifting the mood rather than weighing it down or snarling it up. When you're playing with the boys, especially, it's wise to remember that most of them see life as a game.

Social media is a place to practice this approach. When you find yourself the target of a troll or just a pugnacious "friend," instead of getting huffy, keep it light. Can you make the troll laugh? Can you make the onlookers laugh? It's tricky, because laughing *at* the person—especially if the person is a man—can backfire bigtime. But if you can make him feel you're joining with pleasure in snappy trash-talk with a worthy opponent, an opponent who you're confident will get the jokes, you can often transform the whole thing from mud-brawl to fireworks show. ("I smell sulfur!" as the producer character on *The Larry Sanders Show* used to chortle.) Be generous with the wink/smile emojis, and have fun.

Say "Yes, and . . ." It's the number-one rule of improvisational comedy: always accept the offer. This means that when your skit partner says, "Omg, there's a giant pink rhinoceros at the door!" you don't say, "No way," or "What?" or "How weird." What you say is: "Yes, and it's about time she got here with the pizza!"

A "no" in any form drops the conversational ball. A "yes and" (i.e., accepting the offer) picks up the ball and tosses it back, keeping the rally going. When Sei grabbed a piece of charcoal to write, "Who will come visiting this grass-thatched hut?" she was improvising in the best sense. Her reply was so clever it stunned her adversaries into silence; the story, however, raced around the Japanese court, made it all the way to the emperor, and still has legs today.

This improv technique can be practiced at home. The next time your partner, housemate, or teenager trots out the sarcasm—"Wow, you really love mac 'n' cheese, don't you?"—don't snap back, "No, it's just all I have energy for after a brutal fourteen-hour day." Instead, try a yes-and:

"Yes, in fact the people at Kraft are giving me a special award!"

"Yes, and did you know studies show mac 'n' cheese lovers have the highest IQs?"

"Yes, it's my favorite thing in the world—after washing your socks, of course."

One of the reasons my mother was so popular wherever she went was her ability to talk to anyone: from Soviet ambassadors to Jamaican musicians, from burly US Marines to small Laotian children. I asked her once what her secret was. "I pick up on whatever they say and go with it," she said. She was a practitioner of yes-and.

Be brief. Like the Empress, the Jesteress is a woman of few but well-chosen words. As I noted in the previous chapter, the criticism that women yammer on isn't really fair; studies show that men take up much more airtime than women in most situations. Still, a battle of wits is won quickly. If you find yourself the recipient of verbal jabs and are tempted to launch into a tirade, stop and remember: brevity is the soul of wit.

Or, as Supreme Jesteress Dorothy Parker would have it . . . of lingerie.

12

THE WITCH

THE OLD NURSE HOBBLES ONSTAGE, joints creaking. She faces the audience, all of whom have been buzzing for weeks about this latest play by Euripides, and begins a lament on a theme they know well: Medea, the sorceress from the East who fell in love with Jason and helped him in his quest for the Golden Fleece.

Much more than helped, actually, for it was Medea and Medea alone whom Jason has to thank for his many triumphs—over fire-breathing bulls, a never-sleeping dragon, the sea-monster Scylla, his evil uncle Pelias, the list goes on—and for the couple's safe arrival at last in Corinth, where they've been given sanctuary. Medea of the green-gold eyes left her family and homeland to be with Jason, stopping at nothing to ensure his success. They were married on the long journey back. She is his legal wife and the mother of his two sons.

But now, the nurse says, Jason has got himself another girl: the beautiful young daughter of the king of Corinth. Jason has married this princess—an alliance, he explains, which will be beneficial for him, for the children, and for Medea, too. *Don't worry*, he tells her, *you can stay on as my first concubine. Pretty good deal, eh?*

Medea's reaction is not positive.

The nurse, wise to the ways of her mistress, predicts disaster: "She is dangerous. I know how she responds to treachery. No one who goes against her can win."[1]

Medea: Ruthless in Revenge

Finally we come to Archetype Twelve: the Witch.

Hatred of witches was blown from embers to flame by the sixteenth-century Christian church, but the embers were there even in the old days of paganism. Powerful women, especially those who claim knowledge of the occult, have been feared and despised ever since men turned their worship from earth-goddesses to sky-gods. Although there is no evidence that a truly matriarchal society has ever existed, pre-classical communities did tend to revere women's role in creating life and, hence, their connection to awe-inspiring natural forces. "In the beginning was nature," Camille Paglia writes in her book *Sexual Personae*. And nature is woman.

But if men once perceived women as semi-divine, close to the earth's deep fertile magic in ways they themselves could never be, that view changed when tribal communities began to be replaced by city-states with roads and armies, aqueducts and senates. Manhood was in. Womanhood was out. Fertility cults and priestesses were still around, to be sure, but the "normal" female sphere shrank to the domestic. An unmarried woman who summoned spirits or called on strange energies was stepping far out of her place. While she might have glamour, she was not to be trusted. She was a Witch: the ultimate insubordinate.*

When Jason first meets Medea (this part of the story happens long before the action of Euripides's play), she is a princess of Colchis, a worshipper of Hecate—the goddess of spells and potions—and adept at her magical

---

* Although some men, too, were accused of witchcraft, it was deemed primarily a feminine evil. In outlawing priestesses, the Christian church made it dangerous for women to claim spiritual power of any type.

craft. Jason is a prince of Iolcus on a quest cooked up by his usurping uncle Pelias and backed by the goddess Hera: to find the Golden Fleece and bring it home. He has discovered the prize in Colchis, but Medea's father, King Aeëtes, has set him three seemingly impossible tasks to accomplish before he can claim it. When Jason prays for help, Hera decides to manage the problem by arranging for Medea, who until now has remained resolutely unattached, to fall in love with him. The goddess Aphrodite is also in on the scheme; she dispatches her son Eros to shoot Medea with one of his arrows just as Jason is passing by. Here's how Stephen Fry imagines the scene in his book *Heroes*:

"Jason!"

He saw her.

"Ah, Princess Medea, isn't it? I wonder if you can help me. I'm looking for—"

"I can help you. Come, come with me."

She led him by the hand to the corner of the palace where she kept her shrine to Hecate. She turned to him, her green eyes alight.

"I am going to help you with your three trials . . . I love you, Jason. I love you and will come with you when you return to Greece. I will be by your side, always."[2]

Eros's arrow may have set Medea's heart pounding, but her heart was already a susceptible target, for the Witch **burns with passion**: passion for knowledge, for a cause, for a person. To her, love is no game.* That goal she pursues,

---

* Contrast her attitude with that of her sister the Temptress, for whom love is nothing but a game.

The Witch • 185

she will accomplish; that partner she selects, she will hold. Beware anyone who gets in her way.

Medea is not only a disciple of Hecate but also a granddaughter of the sun-god Helios: she's a fire-princess. When it transpires that Jason's first test is to harness a pair of fire-breathing bulls and make them plow a field, she knows she is in her element. She gives Jason a magic salve she has prepared and tells him to rub it all over his body. When he appears before the crowd gathered to watch the show, he is naked, his skin shining with the oil. The bulls are released and charge toward him, belching flame, but he remains unharmed and the bulls, confused and cowed, allow him to hitch them up. He drives them back and forth, plowing deep furrows as the audience cheers. Medea watches from the royal box, quietly exultant, hotly aroused.

For his second test, Jason sows the plowed field with magic dragon's teeth, from which an army rises up, ready to attack. No worries, for Medea has told him what to do: he throws a rock amid the soldiers, causing each one to believe his neighbor to be the thrower. They turn on one another and fight until all are dead. King Aeëtes pastes on a smile, choking down his frustration; there's one more task, and he's confident Jason will fail at it.

The Witch is **at home in the nonhuman world**; that is, the world of animals, spirits, and forces beyond our ken. She traverses the liminal spaces, the doorways, between the everyday and the extraordinary, connecting the two, gaining power over both. Medea leads Jason to the dark forest grove where the Golden Fleece hangs shining in a tree coiled about by a sleepless dragon. Jason must overcome the dragon in order to pass the final test. On seeing the creature, he's inclined to run; Medea, however, steps forward and stares into its eyes until its head droops, its jaw sags, and it totters. Then she takes a ball of herbs from her bag and shoves it into the drooling mouth. The dragon collapses unconscious. Jason leaps over its bulk and grabs the Fleece. Laughing, the lovers race to the shore where the *Argo* waits, jump aboard, and set sail.

The trip back takes years and is fraught with dangers. Throughout, Medea devotes herself to Jason: no hesitations, no limits. She uses sorcery and strategy to help the Argonauts escape sirens and sea monsters, whirlpools and Wandering Rocks—the latter a name for whitewater rapids so intense they spew flame—the enchantress Circe and a giant robot made of bronze. In some versions of the story, Medea's younger brother is aboard; King Aeëtes comes chasing after them, and when she sees his ship gaining, she slays the boy and tosses his dismembered body into the waves. *Now my father will have to stop and perform his funeral rites*, she says with satisfaction. Jason is appalled, but he doesn't object. Nor does he object when they arrive back home in Iolcus only to find his uncle Pelias with no intention of giving up the throne as promised, whereupon Medea says, *I'll fix it*—and does fix it, by tricking Pelias's daughters into submerging their dad in a (supposedly) magic cauldron. Pelias boils to death. Jason is pleased. But the people blame him as much as Medea for this blood-killing, so the two are forced to flee again. Jason will not get to be king—not of Iolcus, anyway.

Euripides's play opens at this juncture. Jason and Medea have been living in Corinth for some months, having been given sanctuary by King Creon. With them are their two little sons, born on the homeward journey. Jason informs Medea that he has divorced her and married Creon's daughter; this way, he says, he'll eventually be king of Corinth, which will be good for the whole family. Medea flips out, hurling threats, so King Creon decides to exile her. In revenge, she poisons Jason's fiancée, slits the boys' throats, and flees the country—all this, according to older versions of the myth, out of spite. Medea, the mother who murders her own children, was a symbol of unspeakable evil: the Witch to top all witches.

Euripides, however, seems to find the matter more complex. While Medea certainly comes across as vindictive, the play's agon (central debate) portrays Jason as a condescending, ignorant, ungrateful cheater and Medea as a wronged wife with every reason to be furious. When she vents her fury we recoil, yet we can't help but see her side. After Jason has explained at length that she should just get over it—*you'd admire my ingenious plan if you weren't so sex-obsessed*, he sneers—and that anyway he owes her nothing because Aphrodite did all the real work, the Chorus, an objective commenter on the action, remarks: "Jason, reasonable words make reasonable arguments, and I could believe them but truth lies in deeds; and I'm sorry to say, you left Medea."[3] Medea asks why, if this marriage was such a selfless scheme, he kept it secret until now. Why not ask her for help? Jason sneers again: *If I'd divulged my plan, what part of your hateful, broken heart would have helped me?* This exchange follows:

> *Medea:* The part that knows your shame to live the rest of your days with a barbarian like me was greater than your honor.

> *Jason:* I'll say this once more! I didn't need another woman. The marriage was strategic, a defensive ploy to protect you—to give our sons brothers connected to the throne.

> *Medea:* I don't need fortune's gifts if they're made from pain, or wealth derived from the heart's torture.[4]

He stomps away. "Jason will pay for mistreating me," she seethes. When his sons and hideous bride are dead, "who then will dare to say I'm weak or timid? No, they'll say I'm **loyal as a friend, ruthless as a foe**, so much like a hero destined for glory."[5]

She proceeds without hesitation to kill the bride by means of a ghastly gift: a poison robe that burns flesh from bones. Later, though, we see her agonize over the children. She can't do it, she says. Her mother-love is too strong; she must abandon them and go. But then she considers what will befall them: the sons of a barbarian woman, a threat to any half brothers arising from Jason's next marriage, foreign intruders with no protector, not even their father—who, we've seen, lacks both honor and affection. They will end up dead, at far crueler hands than hers. She steels herself. The Chorus calls on her grandfather Helios to stop her: "Brilliant, heavenly light, burn up this murdering Fury"—but he does not stop her. She follows through.*

And when it's all over, Helios sends a flying chariot drawn by dragons so Medea can make her escape. Jason appears, reeling with grief and rage.

---

* I wonder whether acclaimed author Toni Morrison took some inspiration from the story of Medea for her book *Beloved*, in which another mother kills her child in order to save the child from a worse fate.

How could you do it? he screams up at his ex-wife. She is holding the bodies of their sons while suspended high over the stage in a boil of smoke and flame that the Greek audience would surely have taken as an indication of the gods' respect, if not favor. Jason curses her. This is her parting speech:

> Why should I waste time replying to your words? Zeus knows how I saved you and how you repaid me with ingratitude. Did you think that after you betrayed our marriage you'd live a life of ease, mocking me with Creon and his daughter, the princess he promised you before condemning me to exile? Yes, call me fierce and vicious. Say I'm a water fiend like Scylla—tell me, how does it feel with my teeth in your heart?[6]

Loyal as a friend, ruthless as a foe. Deplore the Witch's evil if you want, but recognize also that, come hell or high water, she does what is necessary.

Maddie: Taming Dragons

Maddie was the first real friend I made in boarding school. She had been at St. George's for a year already when I arrived in the fall of 1977 to take a place in the fourth form (tenth grade) of the venerable New England institution. I was assigned a double on the top floor of Astor dormitory; Maddie, unusually for a fourth-former, had a single in the basement. Her room was dim and cozy, with a battered green leather reclining armchair in which I would curl up to do homework, having snuck downstairs to spend evening study hours with her.

The prep school caste system is rigid and all-encompassing. Things may be different today, but back then the formula was *athletic + rich + party-hearty + good-looking.** Hit all four, you were royalty; three, you were popular;

---

* To be considered good-looking, you had to start by being white, slender, and able-bodied.

two, you were accepted; one, you were tolerated; and if you were unlucky enough to hit none, you might as well pin on your Weirdo badge and resign yourself to a lonely life until graduation. Most kids tried desperately to fit in, working with whatever assets they had. I was fairly pretty, but that first year—since I was a shapeless young fourteen, too terrified ever to smile, and determined to wear a pair of contact lenses that made me squint—nobody noticed. For a month I trailed around after some other girls on my hall, sitting with them at meals, listening with silent envy to their chatter, and joining them on the illicit smoking porch where I'd fail to look cool with a cigarette in my mouth.

Then I met Maddie, and things changed.

She was a scholarship student from midtown New York. Her tread was firm, her posture slouchy, her laugh boisterous. Her manner ranged from forthright to belligerent. Of Scottish descent, she had straight dark hair, hazel eyes, delicately pale freckled skin, and a Resting Bitch Face worthy of a Gorgon. She was fairly athletic, but she had no use for team sports so went out for track, which did not count in a hierarchy where field hockey and lacrosse were at the apex. The twangy Southern rock that blared from stereo speakers over the quad she could not abide, preferring instead Tom Lehrer, Boston, Bruce Springsteen, and classical. Only idiots smoked, she said. Her interests included photography, baseball, and old-time male movie stars, along with books of every variety, which she devoured at breakneck speed. She was a talented artist and did marvelous colored-pencil drawings of animals—penguins, hippos, bears—dressed in ballet tutus.

In short, Maddie made no concessions to peer pressure.

I don't recall exactly how or when I met her, but I recall how I felt: *At last, here's somebody I can talk to.* In addition to spending study hours in her room, I started hanging out with her whenever I could. It was a relief to have a friend, but I wouldn't say she made me feel at ease; on the contrary, I often felt a touch apprehensive in her company, not knowing what she might say or do to irritate someone. Since she always spoke her mind and never avoided conflict, she irritated a lot of people. Many of the students gave her a wide berth; the teachers, while appreciating her quick brain, disliked her frequent flouting of authority. She was often in trouble for skipping chapel, a twice-weekly mandatory event; before going myself, I'd arrange blankets and pillows atop her so she'd look like an unmade bed and, with luck, escape the eye of the dorm-monitor who'd be making rounds. She hated, I think, not the physical chapel but the WASP-y, patriarchal tone of the service and the mandate to attend, for when it came to the semi-pagan annual Christmas festival, in which participation was voluntary, she happily dressed as a page and marched into the candlelit dining hall with seven other pages carrying a fake roast pig with an apple in its mouth, all singing at the top of their lungs, "The boar's head in hand bear I, / bedecked with bay and rosemary!"

Her rebellions took various other shapes. In third form she had been bullied by her roommate, a popular preppie girl who eventually went too far and locked her in the closet, whereupon Maddie broke out of the closet and threw the preppie into the hall on her ass, thereby putting a stop to further torments. In fourth form she entered the Pie Race, a 1.1 mile race around campus. She beat all the other girls, including the top athletes, and many of the boys, too, causing shock and dismay among the jock population. But that was the last time she ran the race; she had made her point. Then there was the time in fifth form when she set up an easel and canvas in the common area outside our room (we were roommates that year) and executed an oil painting of the school's headmaster in Nazi uniform and Hitler mustache.

But if Maddie wasn't an easy friend, she was a very good friend. For one thing, she was utterly loyal; although she wouldn't hesitate to *tell* me off, I never worried that she'd *cut* me off. For another, she dragged me out of my comfort zone. One afternoon during a Thanksgiving holiday spent at her place in New York, we took the subway downtown to a second-run cinema to see *The Deer Hunter*, her favorite film, starring Robert De Niro, her favorite actor (this in an era when the Lower East Side was not a place for two teenage girls to be at any time of day). The movie over, we emerged from the theater onto a deserted street. It was dark and drizzling, the streetlights emitting a pale gray glow. We set off for the subway station some blocks east; seeing a man slumped in a doorway, his cigarette tip a spot of fire in the rain, I began to feel scared. Suddenly Maddie stopped and glanced around, lifting her nose as if to sniff the wind. "We ought to get a cab," she said. "This way." She led me quickly to the nearest uptown avenue and hailed a taxi. Looking back on the episode, I know that had I been with anyone but Maddie, things might have taken a dangerous turn; also, had I been with anyone but Maddie, we wouldn't have gone downtown in the first place.

We went to different colleges and lost touch for a while but reunited in our thirties, both of us married by then. She had worked for a law firm then quit to become a full-time mother and, later, a tarot-reader and novel-writer. Today she and her husband, a surgeon, live in a rambling old New England farmhouse stuffed to the brim with books, curios, and cooking paraphernalia. At some point along the way she discovered social media and took to it like a punk rocker to a mosh pit. More feminist than ever, she attacks misogynist trolls as readily as she once manhandled the obnoxious roommate and is constantly getting thrown in Facebook jail for infractions against "community standards." Being liked, for her, is unimportant. Sometimes I want to say *stop being such a loudmouth*—but watching her online has taught me not to fear keyboard warriors. "Mostly," she says, "they're just sad little guys without social skills."

Maddie is also a self-declared witch. Here's how she explains it:

> Strangely, nobody has a clear idea of how the word *witch* was derived or what it was originally supposed to mean. The interpretation that rings most true to me is that *witch* is the ancient European version of *shaman*: one who connects to the spirit realm and can perform healing, magic, and divination. The term is vague and fraught with sociopolitical angst, much of which I think is due to the problematic position such folks have in modern culture. Now, *magic* also has a ton of baggage connected to it, but basically—eye-of-newt aside—it's about the power of words and directed thought-forms to create changes in both the material and spiritual world.

She goes on to say that well-trained witches don't do hexes. "With magical energy, what goes around comes around. If you send out energy forcing someone to do something, expect it to come back on you." What if you want to stop bad people from causing harm? Rather than use negative magic, she says, you can practice protective magic for yourself and others.

Maddie has powerful protective magic. Like Medea, she knows how to block fire-breathing bulls and summon flying chariots; or, put more prosaically, how to keep you safe in New York City. Unlike Medea, she isn't a serial killer; still, to quote the old nurse in Euripides's play, "She is dangerous... No one who goes against her can win." Although she is a Libra, I think she belongs equally to the fire-sign Leo: a lion queen with green-gold eyes. Is anyone really safe with her? Well—as C. S. Lewis says of Aslan—it isn't as if she's a *tame* lion.

Learning from the Witch

Today there are self-proclaimed witches galore, but many of them are (to use Maddie's term) "baby witches," out to snare a lover or punish a nasty boss. The mature Witch doesn't trifle thus; she, more than any of the archetypes, has respect for woman-power and an appreciation of its risks. Here are two ways to tap her strength.

Be judiciously ruthless. Boundaries are necessary to a healthy life, and sometimes boundaries must be enforced without pity—without ruth. Recently I told an old schoolmate to stop ranting on my Facebook page, whereupon he sent me a hostile private message that included an incongruous confession of his "huge crush" on me long ago at St. George's. I replied dismissively. He replied back angrily, calling me "ruthless." Later he apologized, but his insult made me think about the word, what it means, and why I'd sort of enjoyed having it applied to me. I concluded that "ruthless" is what people call women who won't tolerate crap: women who, like

Medea, refuse to be intimidated, sweet-talked, or blackmailed into accepting mistreatment.

Here are four forms of abuse we should ruthlessly reject:

1. **Betrayal.** Medea provides Jason unstinting support, protects him through years of mortal danger, and bears his children—then one day he announces, "I have divorced you. I've married someone new." *Unacceptable*, says Medea.

2. **One-sided fealty.** *I know you're still into me*, says Jason, *so you can stay on as my concubine.* If she takes that deal, Medea will have to be faithful to her ex-husband even as she watches him being unfaithful to her. Although she still adores him, she says *forget it.*

3. **Gaslighting.** *I'm being rational, here*, says Jason. *I'm only thinking of you and the kids. You're the crazy bitch who can't appreciate my plan.* But Medea knows she is on solid ground. *If you were only thinking of me, why not tell me your plan earlier?* she asks, with justification. *I'm not the crazy one.*

4. **Degradation.** "Insane." "Slut." "Stupid." "Hateful." These are the words Jason hurls in public at his broken-hearted wife. Worst of all: "Barbarian." He might as well have called her the n-word. She calmly parries every verbal blow. Then she sets about plotting her revenge. *He'll pay*, she says.

In the killing of her children, we see Medea's ruthlessness carried to an appalling extreme, for which, naturally, no one is advocating. Many of us women, however, are conditioned to go to the other extreme: to sympathize and make excuses for those who abuse us. "He's overworked," we say. "Poor guy, he didn't mean it. I made him angry. I must try harder." These are the words of enablement, and while we shouldn't blame ourselves if we use enablement as a survival strategy, we should label it as just that—a strategy—meanwhile emptying our hearts of pity for the abuser.

When it comes to people who violate our boundaries, we can all do with a bit of Medea's attitude. When we display such an attitude, we should expect to be called ruthless. And we should take it as a compliment.

Heal the rifts. The Witch is an enchantress, but you don't need to practice or even believe in enchantment in the "abracadabra" sense in order to practice her skill—which may seem the opposite of ruthless—in bringing worlds together.

Teacher, astrologer, and author Briana Saussy writes in her book *Making Magic*:

> We are all looking for a way to heal the deepest rifts and fractures of life. The most beautiful, the most magical of all things we can do is to find the means to reframe and unify the deepest discords not only within ourselves but also in our relationships—with other people, with animals, and with our world—to heal our broken planet. I have also found that the greatest rift of all is the one that cuts apart the everyday from the extraordinary.[7]

There are many ways to create this type of healing. One way is to draw clear and firm boundaries, as discussed above, so you're protected from those who wish you harm. But another way is to open your mind and heart to people, ideas, and experiences that seem strange, frightening, even hostile. I might have had better luck with my feisty high-school friend had I first acknowledged his crush confession, for it was no doubt his way of trying to restore some type of link with me, and although I was right to reject his rudeness, I don't think I was right to brush off his sentimental disclosure. *Attend to feelings first* is an old business rule for soothing the angry customer. And everyone—absolutely everyone—has feelings that need soothing. "I understand" can be a magical phrase.

Medea knocked a dragon unconscious, but Maddie once approached a dragon in a more creative way. The mascot of St. George's was, naturally, a dragon. Over the years the school oversaw (or rather, ignored) many abuses of power resulting in private agonies, and I've often thought that the institution's seminal myth—a saintly knight spearing to death a ferocious but ultimately helpless beast—somehow fed that violence and pain. Whether it did or not, I know that a number of us former students are still seeking healing.

In her last semester there, Maddie drew for the school literary magazine a picture of an armored Saint George and a chubby, spike-tailed dragon, both hoisting beer steins, their backs to the viewer as they dance away side by side: two opposed souls united in revelry, their quarrel forgotten. The picture still makes me laugh, and it also makes me wonder how a true Witch would go about taming the dragons in her life. Would she fight them? Hypnotize them? Or would she invite them over for a drink and a song?

THE MASTER MAID

LET'S END WITH A FAIRY TALE.

Versions of "The Master Maid" are found from Scotland to Japan, India to Samoa, Madagascar to North America. In the Aarne-Thompson-Uther Index of folktale types, it is No. 313: The Magic Flight. Andrew Lang, editor of the *Fairy Book* series (*Blue*, *Red*, etc.), picked up his version from folklorists Asbjørnsen and Moe, who in turn had it from Anne Godlid, a famous Norwegian storyteller. Lang offers this as the story's gist:

> A young man is brought to the home of a hostile animal, a giant, cannibal, wizard, or a malevolent king. He is put by his unfriendly host to various severe trials, in which it is hoped that he will perish. In each trial he is assisted by the daughter of his host. After achieving the adventures, he elopes with the girl, and is pursued by her father. The runaway pair throw various common objects behind them, which are changed into magical obstacles and check the pursuit of the father. The myth has various endings, usually happy, in various places.[1]

Lang goes on to say that ATU 313 is "perhaps of all myths the most widely diffused, yet there is no ready way of accounting for its extraordinary popularity."[2] I think the reason for its popularity is evident. Read on for my version, which I've based on several sources, and see whether you agree.

The Master Maid: A New Telling

Once upon a time there was a prince who was so bored with being a prince that he decided to set out into the world to see what else there was. As evening fell on his seventh day of roaming, he came to a large house with a Help Wanted sign on the gate. The householder turned out to be a giant; he was fearsome looking but seemed friendly enough, so the prince (whose name was Manu) put in his application and was hired as a general servant. The giant showed him to his room, a comfortable chamber off the main hall to the left, and bid him goodnight.

The next morning, Manu got up early and went to receive his assignments. The giant said, "I have a small stable that's gotten into a real mess. I want you to muck it out."

"Yes, sir," said Manu. "And after that?"

"After that you may rest or roam about the estate or whatever you like," said the giant, "for you'll find that I'm an easy boss. But listen..." He grinned; *Not a nice grin*, thought Manu. "Under no circumstances may you go through the door that leads off the hall to the right. I absolutely forbid it. And make sure that stable is done before I'm back at sundown, or it will be the worse for you."

"Of course, sir," Manu said. *How weird*, he thought.

The giant left, and naturally the first thing Manu did was go back to the house, into the hall, and through the door on the right. He found himself in a chamber exactly like his, except it contained a young woman sitting on a window bench reading a book.

"Hello," said Manu.

"Hello," said the woman, not looking up.

"Who are you?"

She turned a page. "I'm Sofia. Who are you?"

Manu felt suddenly shy. "My name is Manu. I just hired on as a serv—I mean, as, um, general manager of estate operations. I'm a prince, actually. But I wanted to get some ground-up experience before I take up my, um, prince-dom, because..." He petered out as he saw Sofia's lips twitch with amusement.

She looked up from her book. "Won't you sit down?"

Manu's confidence surged anew. *Hey, maybe I can get somewhere with her*, he thought, and he moved to sit close. But her direct stare discomfited him, and he found himself perched at the other end of the bench.

She kept her dark eyes on him, appraising. After a stretch of silence, she said, "What is my father having you do for your first task?"

"Your—father?"

"The giant is my father."

"Oh! Wow. Does he make you stay in this room all day?"

"Yes. That's his preference, anyway. So, what is he having you do?"

Manu flicked a hand. "Nothing much. He wants me to clean the stable. Hey, how about—" He scooted a bit nearer. "Maybe we could take a walk, get something to eat? There's an alehouse just down the road. Your father wouldn't have to know."

She raised her brows. "Don't you have to do the stable?"

"Sure, but that'll take an hour, tops. He showed me it this morning; it's tiny."

She remained silent, gazing into his eyes. *Hmm*, he thought, *maybe skip the alehouse; she seems really into me.* He allowed himself a quick glance at her chest and eased a little closer—but stopped short when she asked abruptly, "What's my name?"

"Um, sorry?"

"What. Is. My. Name?"

Manu looked down at his knees and searched his mind. He almost couldn't remember, but then: "Sofia. You said it was Sofia." *Sheesh, is this chick nuts?*

"That's right. Very good. All right, Manu, I'm going to tell you something important." She closed her book, put it aside, and turned to face him. "It's a lot harder to clean that stable than you'd think. Lucky for you, I know the secret: you need to turn the shovel around and use the handle—do you hear me, the *handle*—to throw out the straw and dung."

OK, now I know she's nuts, Manu thought. *She's hot, though, so I'll play along.* "The handle; sure, got it. So, whaddaya say? Lunch?"

Sofia looked amused again. "No, thank you. I always have lunch brought in. But you may stay here and keep me company, if you want."

Manu agreed eagerly, and the two spent the rest of the day together, eating, playing chess, and talking. Actually Manu did most of the talking, for Sofia turned out to be an excellent listener, appearing interested in all he had to say about his home, his family, and (for he wanted to show her he was no wuss) his life as a down-to-earth, muck-out-the-stables sort of prince.

As the sun was sinking below the treetops and Sofia was winning yet another chess game (*only because I'm letting her*), she said: "You'd better get to that stable."

"Yeah, I guess so," said Manu. He stretched and stood up. "See you tomorrow?"

"If you like. But don't forget what I said about the handle."

"I won't forget." (*What a fruitcake. Fun, though.*) He took his leave reluctantly and went to the stable. He seized the shovel that was leaning on the wall and set to work—but what was this?! With every scoop of dung and straw he flung out the door, a heap twice the size came flying in, and the faster he shoveled, the faster it came, until he was waist-deep in horse manure. Suddenly he remembered what Sofia had said and, in desperation, turned the shovel around and scooped with the handle, whereupon the muck began to fly out at three times the speed with which it had flown in. In a twinkling, the whole stable was clean as new.

Huh, he thought. *She was right.*

When the giant arrived home that evening, he asked whether the stable was done.

"Yes, sir," said Manu. "It didn't take long."

"Show me," said the giant.

When Manu showed him, the giant frowned and said, "Have you been talking with my Master Maid?"

Manu adopted a wide-eyed look. "Master Maid? What's that?"

"Never mind," growled the giant as he stomped away.

The next morning, the giant ordered Manu to fetch his horse home from the hillside.

"Yes, sir," Manu said. "What shall I do after that?"

"You can take the rest of the day off. Like I told you, I'm an easy boss. But mind what I said about not going into that room to the right of the hall. And make sure my horse is in the stable by sundown. If he isn't, it will be the worse for you." He grinned again, unpleasantly.

"Of course, sir."

As soon as the giant had left, Manu went to Sofia's room and again spent most of the day with her. As before, they ate, talked, and played chess. Manu felt happier than he had in a long time. When Sofia asked him what task her father had set him today, he told her about fetching the horse. "This one will be easy," he said. "I'm great with horses."

"Just like you're great at cleaning stables?"

"Ha-ha, I know, that was so bizarre! Thank you for letting me in on the secret, by the way. I couldn't have done it without you."

"No, you couldn't. And you won't be able to do this, either. I'd better come with you."

"What? Nah. I told you, with horses, I know what I'm doing." He ventured to pat her hand. (*Cute how she worries. She's so into me.*)

Sofia rolled her eyes. "No, Manu, listen to me. It's no ordinary horse."

"So it's a little wild. I'm telling you, I can handle it."

"It shoots fire from its nostrils."

"Like I said, I can handle—wait. It does what?"

"Shoots fire. Enormous jets of flame. If you don't know what to do, you'll be fried."

Upon reflection, Manu decided it might indeed be best if Sofia came with him. She packed a bag with some cheese-and-tomato sandwiches and a bridle; Manu asked her to put his spurs in the bag, too, to which she agreed with another eye roll. They set off for the hillside and soon spied the horse grazing in a sunny meadow. It looked like an ordinary horse. As they approached it glanced up at them, still chewing, brown eyes mild.

"He seems harmless enough," said Manu. "I doubt I'll need the spurs after all."

He strode forward, but Sofia grabbed his collar: "*Don't!*" Two jets of flame blasted forth. Had Manu been a step closer, he'd have been toast.

"*Holy shit!*" He stumbled backward and nearly fell on his rear.

"I warned you."

"OK, yes, you warned me! Son of a—what do I do?"

Sofia rummaged in her bag and took out the bridle with its iron bit. She untangled it, saying, "All you need to do is throw the bit straight in his face. As long as your aim is decent, it'll lodge in his mouth, and then he'll be tame as a kitten. Is your aim decent?"

"I guess," said Manu. His head swam and he wasn't sure about anything anymore.

"I know you can do it," said Sofia. She patted his shoulder and handed him the bridle with a dazzling smile. "Just throw it right at him."

With his head even swimmier, Manu took the bit in his hand and, before he could think and change his mind, wound up and hurled it at the horse's head. *Chunk* went the bit. The horse reared up with a mighty *neigh*—then dropped back to the ground and stood still. With Sofia's encouragement, Manu approached and grabbed the bridle. No more flames. They led the placid horse home, sharing the sandwiches that Sofia produced from her bag.

As evening fell, the giant arrived back. "Where's my horse? Not here? I suppose you couldn't manage him, eh?" His eyes narrowed.

"Oh, yes, sir," said Manu. "He's in the stable, as you instructed. He gave me no trouble."

"Hmph," said the giant, scowling. "I *know* you've been talking with my Master Maid."

"Master Maid? I do wish you'd tell me what that is, sir!"

"I bet you do. Well . . . I've another task for you tomorrow."

The next morning, the giant led Manu to a far edge of the estate, where grew a tall tree—and when I say tall, I mean *tall*. Manu craned his neck to see the top, but it was hidden by clouds.

"Three miles high," said the giant, again with that nasty grin.

"Amazing." Manu wondered if he'd have to cut it down.

"At the top there's a nest with three eggs in it. I have a hankering for soft-boiled eggs for my supper. I want you to climb the tree and bring down the eggs. Think you can do that?"

Manu gulped. "No problem."

"Good, good. Now be sure to have them for me when I get back at sundown. And remember…" He leaned in close, breathing his fetid breath in Manu's face. "…if I find out you've been talking to my Master Maid, it will be the worse for you!"

This time, Manu fairly ran to find Sofia. He told her about the tree and the nest and the eggs and begged her to help him. She told him to relax, there was plenty of time; they might as well have a few games of chess first. But Manu insisted they do it *now*, so off they went to the three-mile-high tree and stood at its base, gazing upward.

"How the *hell* am I going to get up there? Wait, I know! I'll just find some other eggs, some hen's eggs, and give him those."

Sofia sighed. "The eggs up there are nothing like hen's eggs. He'll know the difference."

"Fine! What's your idea, then?"

She looked at him: a long, steady look. Then she bent, pulled a small silver knife out of her boot, laid her left hand on the tree trunk, and sliced off her index finger.

"*OH MY GOD!*" Manu screamed. "*What are you doing?*" He lunged to stop her, but Sofia kicked him hard in the shin and he fell back with a yelp.

"Stop screeching," she said, continuing to slice off her fingers one by one. "Just wait."

He leaned down to rub his shin, wincing in pain. The fingers dropped to the ground, and when all ten of them were off (he didn't see how she managed the thumbs, nor did he see any blood) she told him to gather them and stack them in a pile against the tree trunk. He did as she said. Once the stack was made, she told him to stand back, and with her hands in the pockets of her dress she began to sing a low, sweet song, rising higher and higher in pitch until it sounded like birdsong. As she sang, the pile of fingers transformed into a tiny set of stairs, which began to grow, and grow, and wind around the trunk, and in five minutes there was a spiral staircase climbing gracefully up, up, up, around the tree and into the clouds.

"There you go," she said.

"But... but... your fingers..." Manu was trembling.

"Don't worry. As soon as you're done, I'll reattach them. Go on, now."

He felt sick, but he started up the stairs, holding onto the railing. It took him two hours to get to the top, where he found the nest and gathered the eggs, putting them in his side pouch; they were streaked with brilliant red, blue, brown, and green—not the least like hen's eggs. Another hour to get back down, where he found Sofia, hands still in pockets, sitting on the lowest step waiting for him. He showed her the eggs, whereupon she stood, raised her chin, and uttered a sharp command. The spiral staircase dissolved into mist, and look!—there was the pile of fingers at the bottom of the tree. She took her hands out of her pockets and reached down. Then she turned to face him, laughing, wiggling her fingers, all ten of them in place.

Manu seized her hands in his, nearly crying with relief. She leaned forward and kissed him. He kissed her back. They kissed for a long time.

But in the midst of the kissing, one of the eggs broke.

"Uh-oh," said Sofia, as Manu reached into his pouch and pulled out the dripping yellow mess. "That's not good. My father will kill you. We have to get out of here."

"Yes, yes," said Manu, wiping his hand on his tunic. "Let's go! We can go to my parents' place. We can get married there. I mean, um, if you want to."

Sofia smiled her dazzling smile. "Yes. I want to."

So off they went. Sofia insisted on first stopping by her room, where she found a comb, a flask of water, and a chunk of salt, and put them in her bag. Manu asked her why, but she said only, "We'll need them." Then they went out the gate and down the road, heading east. They had been walking for half an hour when they heard a roar and, turning to look, saw the giant, silhouetted against the setting sun, coming after them with a great spiked club.

"Run!" shouted Manu. But Sofia instead reached into her bag, took out the comb, and threw it down in the road behind them. An immense hedge of thorns sprang up, blocking the road and the landscape for a mile on either side. Then she grabbed his hand, and the two ran on, the giant's howls of frustration ringing in their ears.

In the twilight they came to a stream with a rowboat on the bank, and rested awhile. When they heard roars again, they jumped into the boat and Manu began to row—but before they were even a quarter of the way across, the giant hove into view, brandishing his club. "We're sunk!" cried Manu, but Sofia reached into her bag and pulled out the water flask. Just as the giant set foot in the stream, she uncorked the flask and threw it overboard. Instantly the stream swelled into a wide lake, with their boat in the middle and the giant left standing on the edge.

Manu dropped his head and exhaled. When he looked up again, he saw the giant coming after them in a giant-size ship with giant-size sails. *Where on earth did he get the ship?* he wondered, but there was no time to lose in wondering; as he reapplied himself to the oars, he could see their foe gaining on them. "Faster!" Sofia cried, and he thought: *She's out of tricks—this is it.* He threw everything he had into rowing, and the boat flew across the lake until they were fifty . . . forty . . . thirty feet from shore. Sofia had turned to face the giant's ship, which kept gaining; at last, with just twenty feet to their goal, she threw the chunk of salt into the water. A craggy white mountain loomed across the lake, pushing out two great waves on either side. The wave on the lovers' side lifted their boat and propelled it with a *whoosh* high onto the bank, while the wave on the giant's side rose up, curled over, and crashed down upon the ship, driving it and its occupant to the bottom.

Manu and Sofia fell into each other's arms and stayed there for a long time, drenched and panting as the moon rose. When their breath slowed and Manu thought they could go on, he stood and held out his hand to her. But she shook her head and said he should continue to the palace without her, for she needed to perform funeral rites for her father.

"But he was a monster," Manu said. "He kept you prisoner. He tried to kill us both."

"I know. But he was my father, and I owe him this." She rubbed her forehead. "Go now, my dear. I'll come in three days. Don't worry, I'll be fine."

Manu protested, said he would stay with her, but she insisted she must do it alone. Finally he kissed her, said "I love you," and walked away toward the path that led through the forest.

"Manu!" she cried.

"Yes?" He looked back, hoping she had changed her mind.

"What's my name?"

He laughed. "Sofia!"

"That's right. Don't forget it!"

"Of course I won't. See you soon!" He waved, turned, and entered among the trees, sad to leave her yet filled with joy. *How silly*, he thought as he walked along with the moonlight filtering through the canopy. *How could I possibly forget the name of the woman I love, the woman I'm going to marry?*

When he arrived home around midnight, the king and queen rushed to embrace him. They were thrilled to have him back, exclaimed at his bedraggled state, and insisted that he wash and get a good night's sleep before telling them of his adventures. The next morning he awoke refreshed. At the breakfast table he launched into his tale: the fearsome giant, the impossible tasks, the wonderful girl who'd helped him, and their perilous flight. He was so caught up in the telling (and, truth be told, in embellishing his own part in the story) that he didn't notice his parents exchanging worried looks.

When he paused for breath, his mother said: "It all sounds *marvelous*, dear. Such a time you've had! Now, this girl, this Master Maid. What did you say her name was?"

He opened his mouth to speak, and ... *What's her name? I know it! C'mon, I know it! It's ...* His mouth hung open, his mind a blank.

"Hmm," said his father. "Now, look, son; don't take this the wrong way, but are you sure you didn't *dream* this girl? And the giant, and the, what was it? Fire-breathing horse?"

"Trees can't grow three miles high, dear," said his mother.

"This one did! I *saw* it, and I saw *her*! We played chess! We're getting married!" Manu squeezed his eyes shut in desperation. *We're getting married. I'm marrying . . . whatshername.*

For a few hours he continued to insist it was all true, had all happened, but eventually his parents' questions, chuckles, and raised eyebrows sowed seeds of doubt, and he began to wonder whether they were right. The whole adventure, he had to admit, had been awfully dreamlike. And he could not, for the life of him, remember the Master Maid's name. *I guess I did imagine her*, he thought finally. He retired to his room and sat on his bed, head in hands.

On the third day at twilight, Sofia knocked at the palace door. She asked to see the prince, but in her grubby state she was taken for a beggar. She pleaded with the door warden: "Tell him it's Sofia!" But the warden only sneered and told her to get lost.

She went sadly down the drive and, feeling thirsty, wandered over to the well and had a drink of water. Then she climbed a nearby tree and sat on a branch, thinking.

As the full moon rose, to the well came the palace scullery maid, heavy-hearted as usual, longing for a better life. She looked into the well as she lifted the bucket, and there reflected in the water she saw a face—a beautiful, courageous face, which she took for her own.

"Goodness," she said aloud, "if I'm so bonny, if I'm so brave, why should I spend my days washing dishes? I deserve more!" She dropped the bucket and made up her mind to go to the cook right then and give notice, but suddenly she heard a *thud*, and she spun round to see a woman in a tattered dress, her hair twiggy, her face the same as the face in the well.

"Who are you?" gasped the scullery maid.

"I'm Sofia," said Sofia. "Listen. If I help you get what you want, will you help me?"

"I . . . I guess so," said the scullery maid, thinking this was no doubt a dream so she might as well play along.

"Good. Then here's what I need you to do . . ."

Sofia got the scullery maid (whose name was Daisy) to sneak her through a back door and into the palace kitchen, where she spent the night curled up in a corner. Very early the next morning, before any of the other servants were about, she rose, drew the two unbroken eggs out of her bag, removed them from the cotton-wool in which she'd wrapped them, and boiled them hard. She gave them to Daisy, who promised to place them in the covered dish that would be served to the prince. Then she hid in an alcove off the dining room and waited.

Manu came down to breakfast, dejected as he had been for the past three days. His parents were there already and greeted him cheerily. He mumbled "good morning" and took his seat. The footman placed the dish in front of him and lifted the cover—to reveal the two boiled eggs, streaked with brilliant red, blue, brown, and green.

"*Sofia!*" Manu leaped to his feet.

"*Manu!*" She ran to him, smiling her dazzling smile.

They were married in the spring. Sofia asked Daisy to be her personal lady's maid; Daisy proved to have a remarkable talent for chess and, with Sofia as her coach, went on to become a regional champion. The king and queen, having seen how well their son and daughter-in-law did together, decided to retire early and move to the seaside. The realm was left in the capable hands of Manu and Sofia, who lived happily ever after.

◆ ◆ ◆

You've probably noticed the similarities between this myth and the myth of Jason and Medea—in which another "master maid" uses magic to help her lover complete three difficult tasks, only to be forgotten by him when they arrive home—and indeed, Lang speculates that "The Golden Fleece" is the original of ATU 313, from which sprang all other versions. Lang doesn't think it plausible that such a story, with no obvious connection to universal natural phenomena, could have sprung up independently in multiple parts of the world. He believes there was one original legend that was spread from place to place over centuries by women who, subject to the laws of exogamy, were married off into other tribes, bringing with them the tales of their childhood. In other words, Lang envisions a three-thousand-year global game of whisper-down-the-lane.

I'm not so sure about that. It seems to me that ATU 313 is an *archetypal woman's tale*: a heroine's journey that any woman anywhere might spin from her own experience in order to prepare her young sisters for the trials of adult life. As brides were sent from nation to nation, the myriad versions of this primal woman's tale would have collided, blending and evolving until originals and copies were no longer distinguishable. To support this explanation, I note four common elements of the story: elements that Lang seems to have missed, or perhaps considered unimportant, since he left them out of his summary.

The first element is the obvious **leadership** of the Master Maid. She does far more than "assist" the young man in his tasks: she performs feats of magic that mark her as a powerful sorceress, and she directs her lover in ways that leave no doubt of her superior intellect, will, and foresight. She is not the rescued, but the rescuer.

The second element is the Master Maid's **imprisonment**. The father figure* holds her captive, keeps her hidden from view, and refers to her as "mine." Although she has power enough to leave on her own, she has nowhere to go; so, instead of fleeing, she waits calmly for the arrival of a worthy companion. When the two do run away, the father-god pursues them in a rage. I take him to be a symbol of the patriarchy: controlling, abusive, vengeful.

The third element is **dismemberment**: sometimes performed by the Master Maid on another (as when Medea kills and chops up her young brother then tosses his body parts overboard) but more often, and more interestingly, self-inflicted. In my telling I follow the Scottish variant,† in which our heroine cuts off her fingers to form a stairway up the tree. In the Samoan version, she instructs the prince to hack her to pieces and throw the pieces into the sea, where she reconsolidates as a fish, allowing her to complete the third task of finding a ring that the evil being has hidden on the seafloor. Sometimes a tossed comb or hairpin stands in for body parts. Always, the harm to the woman is temporary and unbothersome: she rends herself apart,

---

* In a few versions, the evil being is female: either the girl's mother or some sort of maleficent hag.
† Sometimes titled "Nicht Nought Nothing"

transforms the parts into what she needs, and puts herself back together with a nonchalant agility that gives new meaning to the word *multitask*.

The fourth and final common element is **the man's forgetting** of the woman and, later, her ingenuity and persistence in restoring his memory. Across multiple versions there are multiple ways she does this; often, her fiancé is about to marry another when she finally succeeds in breaking the spell. I especially like the versions (which include Scottish and Malagasy) wherein the Master Maid sits in a tree above water, causing a servant girl to mistake the reflected face for her own, question her own servitude, and offer to help her beleaguered sister.

The male folklorists' summary of ATU 313 goes something like this: "A hero performs dangerous tasks with assistance from a pretty girl who is madly in love with him; he elopes with her, defeating her angry father and finally bringing her to his home."

How might a woman summarize it? "An enchantress directs and protects a young man in performing dangerous tasks set by her abusive father; she engineers their escape using magical objects and later, when the young man forgets her, finds a way to restore his memory."

With the second summary in mind, we can easily clear up Lang's puzzlement about the myth's "extraordinary popularity": ATU 313 is the only ancient myth in which the female protagonist is in no way subordinate, but rather the leader, heroine, and savior. Women in all times and places, I think, have used this story or something like it as a vehicle to share the following wisdom:

- You will be more intelligent than many men and will need to give them direction. To ensure they accept this direction, you must package it as "assistance."
- You will find yourself controlled and held back by the patriarchy; to break free, you must ally with men, but be judicious about whom you ally with.
- Many a time you will have to tear yourself in pieces—literally, when it comes to childbirth, and figuratively, when it comes to

accomplishing everything you must accomplish. Afterward, you will pull yourself together and move on.

- ◆ You'll need support from other women. You should accept their help, and help them in return.
- ◆ Your male associates are likely to "forget" you: to ignore, disdain, and mistreat you. If you want to stay allied with them, you must "remind" them who you are.

Can you hear it? The chorus of women down the ages saying to their daughters and granddaughters, sisters and nieces and friends: "These things are hard, but you can do them—you can do them, because you are the Master Maid."

Learning from the Master Maid

She is mistress of the four elements. In her clearing of the stable, we see earth; in her taming of the horse, fire; in her building of the tree-stair, air; in her creation of the lake, water. In other versions of the story, we find a fiery demon, a lake to be drained, a ring in the ocean, a field to be plowed, a flying carriage, or something else; in each case, the four elements are present and our heroine glides from one to the next, reveling in the challenges they present and in her ability to manage them.

Thus inspired, we can discern four Master Maid principles:

Stand firm. Like the Amazon, Claimant, and Mama Bear, plant your feet and stand assured. Assert your expertise. Know what you know. Rest established in the self. Don't let anyone turn you from your purpose or cause you to doubt your judgment. (Earth)

Flow through. Like the Amiga, Mesmerist, and Empath, accept reality and adapt to it. Bend like a reed in the rain; flow like a stream among rocks. Apply smiles and sympathy, knowing they are not weakness, for in softness there is strength. (Water)

Fly high. Like the Escapist, Snow Queen, and Empress, declare your independence. If you want to disengage, disengage. If you want to take charge, take charge. When it's time to leave, leave: even with a broken wing, show them how you can soar. (Air)

Shine bright. Like the Jesteress, Witch, and Temptress, light the way. Be a beacon in the darkness. Encourage others, by example and word, to achieve more than they thought they could. Bring people together; make them laugh; make them stars. (Fire)

Today, we women are told to succeed by "leaning in." But leaning in is too often like slogging through a bog: all you do is get stuck, tired, and dirty. Rather than lean in, apply the principles above: stand firm, flow through, fly high, shine bright.

You can probably think of times when you have, consciously or not, used one or more of these principles to help you navigate barriers and get where you want to go. For me, it was the time (described in chapter 9) when I realized that in order to move up at my company, I'd have to step out onstage and teach, not just design, training workshops—something that did not come easily to me. I'd have to descend from the Snow Queen's aeries and be, or at least act like, a Temptress and a Mesmerist: to smile, to sparkle, to entertain and engage. At the same time, however, I knew I could rely on my frosty powers: I could prepare better than anyone, take the darts of audience criticism, and speak with an authority born of careful study. With the Snow Queen at my core, I could emulate the virtues of other archetypes, inhabiting their spaces if only for a time. With an ice palace as my base camp, I could embark on a heroine's quest into warmer territories.

You can do the same. If you're an Amazon, you can learn to keep your head down (sometimes) and avoid the fray. A Mama Bear can learn to let the cubs (sometimes) sort out their own problems. An Empress can build relationships. An Empath can put herself first. An Escapist can remain in the game. A Temptress can cool it.

In short, we can all learn to turn the wheel even as we remain true to ourselves.

How do you know which archetype to channel at which time? I'm afraid there is no formula, but I can say for certain: what got you here won't get you there. When you find yourself facing an unfamiliar challenge or opportunity, pushed out of your comfort zone and disoriented in the storm, old habits will not do. In order to move forward, you'll need to adopt some new behaviors and mindsets. Happily, there are lots of role models out there, both real and fictional, from whom you can take a cue. This book has presented some; no doubt you can find many more.

Seek out the Empress, Mama Bear, and Temptress; the Empath, Amazon, and Escapist; the Mesmerist, Claimant, and Snow Queen; the Amiga, Jesteress, and Witch. Watch them. Learn from them. Draw upon their strengths.

Lean in? No. Range wide. Woman is born free, and there are a thousand ways to break the chains.

POSTSCRIPT

"THIS IS A CLEAR CASE of insubordination."

The lawyer's voice on the phone was harsh. It was the morning of January 30, 2013, and I was being fired. The details don't matter now; suffice to say I had made the mistake of letting my bosses know just how much I disdained them, so I'd become persona non grata. In a companywide meeting convened that afternoon, employees were instructed not to talk to me lest they, too, be terminated. "We were threatened with pink slips," someone told me later.

In the days that followed I received not five, not twenty, but *seventy* phone calls, emails, cards, and messages from women colleagues—plus more than a few "honorary women" (as my friend Maggie calls enlightened men)—all of whom wanted to make sure I was OK and to wish me well. In the wake of my insubordination, nearly half the firm was insubordinate for my sake. But while my insubordination had consisted, essentially, of a Medusa's scornful glare, my colleagues' insubordination was something far nobler: Amazons and Amigas, Mama Bears and Mesmerists, Empresses and Escapists reached out and, each in her own way, helped me through a tough time. Some listened to me rant, some joked, some advised, some offered practical assistance, some simply said "we miss you." There were even a few folks who I know for a fact didn't like me much (well, I *was* uptight and unfriendly!) yet broke ranks and contacted me, just to say they were sorry to see me go.

And in the years since, I've been sustained by that gang of insubordinate women, actual and honorary. They've hoisted me out of Medusa Traps in which I was foundering and encouraged me to try again. They've taught me that defeating the patriarchal giant really does take a village, or perhaps a fairy book, of diverse characters pulling together. They've shown me how to pick up the pieces, stick them back on, and forge ahead. Even as I write this, they are standing firm . . . flowing through . . . flying high . . . shining bright.

They are the Master Maids: bonny, brave leaders. I am grateful to them, one and all.

APPENDIX

Do's and Don'ts for Each Archetype

Archetype	Do	Don't
1. Temptress	• Make people feel special • Bring the fun • Let them see you like them	• Hog the spotlight • Ghost people who've lost your interest • Violate boundaries
2. Amazon	• Know what you want • Find allies • Be sure in your rightness • Fight with good intent	• Fight for the sake of fighting • Stop listening • Make relationships about power
3. Claimant	• Strengthen your BATNA • Play by the rules	• Claim what isn't yours • Rest on your reputation • Fail to make an exit plan

Archetype	Do	Don't
4. Mama Bear	• Identify with your team's success • Treat them differently • Take the blame	• Hang everything on your "kids" • Micromanage • Overindulge your favorites
5. Amiga	• See relationships in two dimensions (friend or foe, ally or adversary)	• Mistake allies for friends • Mistake adversaries for foes • Try to please everyone
6. Mesmerist	• Persist... nicely • Emphasize larger goals • Give your audience space	• Seek only to manipulate • Sell past the close • Count on your charm
7. Empath	• Listen and confirm • Err toward generosity • Be an objective eye	• Get caught up in their drama • Play the martyr • Ignore your own needs
8. Escapist	• Disengage • Learn to say "No" • Embrace the gift of fear	• Give up too soon • Apologize for nothing • Refuse all risk
9. Snow Queen	• Expect commitment • Focus on results • Keep calm and carry on	• Ignore people's feelings • Take devotion for granted • Take yourself too seriously
10. Empress	• Respect the hierarchy • Speak with conviction • Push for your purpose • Lean in—literally	• Rely on positional authority • Confuse power with happiness • Underestimate the meek
11. Jesteress	• Take fights lightly • Say "Yes, and..." • Be brief	• Use mockery as a weapon • Forget to be kind • Be indiscreet
12. Witch	• Be judiciously ruthless • Heal the rifts	• Assume you know it all • Let anger take over • Flout the rules for the hell of it

ACKNOWLEDGMENTS

MOST OF ALL I WANT to thank the twelve women who served as real-life examples in these pages. You are my muses. I hope you recognize yourselves and forgive me: first for putting you in a box, second for presenting, along with your many admirable qualities, a few foibles. (All praise makes for dull reading.)

Inbar Fried did an incredible job with the illustrations. I knew she was right for the project when I first saw her beautiful pen-and-ink drawings of women and trees. She saw the vision and traveled with me the whole way.

The Forum Corporation, the Boston-based consulting and training firm where I worked for some 25 years, continues to be a source of wisdom for my writings on leadership and life. The same is true of St. John's College, Santa Fe, where I earned my MA in Eastern classics and where I first encountered several of my literary examples of the archetypes.

My thanks go to Ted Higgins and Emily Davis, who read early sections of the manuscript and provided valuable input, and to the team at Amplify Publishing, who shepherded the book to market.

Finally, to my dear friends and family—especially Sylvia, Maggie, and Matt—I can never adequately express my gratitude for your steadfast, loving support during the events to which I allude in chapter 7. It was a terrible, horrible, no-good, very bad time. Now it's material. You made that possible.

ABOUT THE AUTHOR
AND ILLUSTRATOR

JOCELYN DAVIS is an internationally known author and speaker and the former head of R&D for a global leadership development consultancy. Her previous business books include *Strategic Speed, The Greats on Leadership,* and *The Art of Quiet Influence.* Her latest is a historical novel, *The Age of Kali,* called "brilliant," "heretical," and "deeply moving." Jocelyn holds master's degrees in philosophy and Eastern classics. She grew up in a foreign-service family living in many regions of the world, including Southeast Asia, East Africa, and the Caribbean. Currently she lives in Santa Fe, New Mexico. Visit her website at JocelynRDavis.com.

INBAR FRIED is an artist and freelance illustrator working in several different mediums. She was born and raised on a kibbutz in the middle of the Negev desert and now resides in Jerusalem. As her own archetype, she identifies strongly with the Escapist.

ENDNOTES

The Heroine's Journey

1 Rosa Brooks, "Recline, don't 'Lean In' (Why I hate Sheryl Sandberg)," *Washington Post*, Feb. 25, 2014.

2 Quoted with the author's permission.

Chapter One

1 Henri Meilhac and Ludovic Halévy, *Carmen: An Opera in Four Acts*, composed by Georges Bizet, translated by Lionel Salter, New York: The Metropolitan Opera, 1973, compact disc. Print libretto, page 35.

2 Meilhac, *Carmen*, 33.

3 Meilhac, *Carmen*, 35.

4 Meilhac, *Carmen*, 53.

5 Meilhac, *Carmen*, 59.

6 Meilhac, *Carmen*, 65.

7 Meilhac, *Carmen*, 85.

8 Meilhac, *Carmen*, 49.

9 Meilhac, *Carmen*, 109.

10 Meilhac, *Carmen*, 143.

11 Meilhac, *Carmen*, 147.

Chapter Two

1   Aristophanes, *Lysistrata and Other Plays*, translated by Alan H. Sommerstein (London: Penguin Random House UK, 2002), line 250.
2   Aristophanes, *Lysistrata and Other Plays*, 212-224.
3   Aristophanes, *Lysistrata and Other Plays*, preface.
4   Aristophanes, *Lysistrata and Other Plays*, 100.
5   Aristophanes, *Lysistrata and Other Plays*, 112.
6   Aristophanes, *Lysistrata and Other Plays*, 165.
7   Aristophanes, *Lysistrata and Other Plays*, 733.
8   Aristophanes, *Lysistrata and Other Plays*, 145.
9   Aristophanes, *Lysistrata and Other Plays*, 350-368.
10 Aristophanes, *Lysistrata and Other Plays*, 372-377.
11 Aristophanes, *Lysistrata and Other Plays*, 495-499.
12 Aristophanes, *Lysistrata and Other Plays*, 510-525.
13 Aristophanes, *Lysistrata and Other Plays*, 1015.
14 This bit of verse may have been printed originally in *The Boston Evening Transcript*, a daily afternoon newspaper published in Boston from 1830 to 1941.
15 Aristophanes, *Lysistrata and Other Plays*, 650.

Chapter Three

1   The Mahabharata, *The Book of the Beginning*, translated by J. A. B. van Buitenen, (Chicago: University of Chicago Press, 1973), 166.
2   The Mahabharata, 164.
3   The Mahabharata, 166.
4   The Mahabharata, 166.
5   The Mahabharata, 167.
6   The Mahabharata, 168.
7   The Mahabharata, 169.
8   The Mahabharata, 170.

Chapter Four

1   The Bible, Revised Standard Version, (New York: Meridian, 1974), copyright 1962 by The World Publishing Company.

Chapter Five

1 The story of Savitri is found in the Mahabharata, *The Book of the Forest*, chapter 42. Translations from the Sanskrit are my own. I am indebted to St. John's College tutor emeritus Bruce Perry for his Sanskrit glossary of the story.

2 The Relationship Types graphic is my own. The concept of the two axes and the four types comes from Laurence J. Stybel and Maryanne Peabody, "Friend, Foe, Ally, Adversary . . . or Something Else?," *MIT Sloan Management Review* 46, no. 4 (June 2005).

Chapter Six

1 My source for the Shahrazad story and all quotations is Amabel Williams-Ellis, *The Arabian Nights* (London and Glasgow: Blackie & Son, Limited, 1957).

2 Williams-Ellis, *The Arabian Nights*, 15–16.

3 Williams-Ellis, *The Arabian Nights*, 18.

4 Joe Fassler, "The Humanist Message Hidden Amid the Violence of *One Thousand and One Nights*," *The Atlantic*, June 25, 2013.

5 Fassler, "The Humanist Message."

6 Williams-Ellis, *The Arabian Nights*, 322.

7 Williams-Ellis, *The Arabian Nights*, 322.

8 Sheryl Sandberg, *Lean In: Women, Work, and the Will to Lead* (New York: Alfred A. Knopf, 2013).

Chapter Seven

1 My source for the Miaoshan/Guanyin story, details on its historical background, and all quotations is Glen Dudbridge, *The Legend of Miaoshan* (Oxford University Press, 1978).

2 Dudbridge, *The Legend of Miaoshan*, 31.

3 Dudbridge, *The Legend of Miaoshan*, 32.

4 Dudbridge, *The Legend of Miaoshan*, 33.

5 Dudbridge, *The Legend of Miaoshan*, 12.

6 Dudbridge, *The Legend of Miaoshan*, 26.

7 Dudbridge, *The Legend of Miaoshan*, 28.

8 Dudbridge, *The Legend of Miaoshan*, 25.

9   Dudbridge, *The Legend of Miaoshan*, 30.

Chapter Eight

1   Homer, *The Odyssey*, translated by Robert Fagles (New York: Penguin Books, 1996), 96.

2   Homer, *The Odyssey*, 97.

3   Homer, *The Odyssey*, 370.

4   Homer, *The Odyssey*, 371.

5   Homer, *The Odyssey*, 384.

6   Homer, *The Odyssey*, 409.

7   Homer, *The Odyssey*, 459.

8   Homer, *The Odyssey*, 461.

9   Homer, *The Odyssey*, 462.

10   Homer, *The Odyssey*, 463.

11   Gavin de Becker, *The Gift of Fear: Survival Signals That Protect Us from Violence* (self-pub., 1997).

12   De Becker, *The Gift of Fear*, ch. 11.

Chapter Nine

1   Richard Wagner, *Tristan Und Isolde: Opera in Three Acts*, translator unknown, London: The Royal Opera House, Covent Garden, 1953, compact disc. Print libretto, page 53.

2   Wagner, *Tristan Und Isolde*, 63.

3   Wagner, *Tristan Und Isolde*, 79.

4   Wagner, *Tristan Und Isolde*, 81.

5   Wagner, *Tristan Und Isolde*, 101.

6   Wagner, *Tristan Und Isolde*, 103.

7   Wagner, *Tristan Und Isolde*, 109.

8   Wagner, *Tristan Und Isolde*, 113.

9   Wagner, *Tristan Und Isolde*, 253.

10   Jocelyn Davis, *The Art of Quiet Influence: Timeless Wisdom for Leading without Authority* (London/Boston: Nicholas Brealey Publishing, 2019), 165.

Chapter Ten

1   All quotations are from William Shakespeare's *Macbeth*, Bantam Books edition, 1988.

Chapter Eleven

1   Sei Shonagon, *The Pillow Book*, translated by Meredith McKinney (New York: Penguin Books, 2006), 67.

2   Sei Shonagon, *The Pillow Book*, 67.

3   Sei Shonagon, *The Pillow Book*, ix.

4   Sei Shonagon, *The Pillow Book*, 66.

5   Sei Shonagon, *The Pillow Book*, xvi.

6   Sei Shonagon, *The Pillow Book*, 67.

7   Sei Shonagon, *The Pillow Book*, 68.

8   Sei Shonagon, *The Pillow Book*, 69.

9   Sei Shonagon, *The Pillow Book*, 316.

10 Sei Shonagon, *The Pillow Book*, 69.

11 Zara Bentley Roberts, private correspondence, January 9, 1980.

Chapter Twelve

1   Euripides, *Medea*, translated by Michael Collier and Georgia Machemer (Oxford University Press, 2006), lines 35–37.

2   Stephen Fry, *Heroes: The Greek Myths Reimagined* (San Francisco, CA: Chronicle Books, 2018), 193.

3   Fry, *Heroes*, 584–586.

4   Fry, *Heroes*, 599–608.

5   Fry, *Heroes*, 795–802.

6   Fry, *Heroes*, 1325–1334.

7   Briana Saussy, *Making Magic: Weaving Together the Everyday and the Extraordinary* (Boulder, CO: Sounds True, 2019), 10.

The Master Maid

1   Andrew Lang, "A Far-Travelled Tale," in *Custom and Myth* (Longmans, Green and Co., 1884), 87–102, accessed at https://en.wikisource.org/wiki/Custom_and_Myth/A_Far-Travelled_Tale.

2   Lang, "A Far-Travelled Tale."